EXTRAORDINARY WOMEN BY GRACE

MARY WHELCHEL

CHRISTIAN FOCUS

You hold in your hands a book that can transform the life of anyone---no matter how serious their failures or how stubborn their sins! I was intrigued by these stories because I know that they describe real women who encountered real grace, forgiveness and transformation. If anyone doubts that God can redeem our failures, they should read this book, then pass it along to a friend!

Erwin W. Lutzer
The Moody Church, Chicago

© MARY WHELCHEL

ISBN 1-84550-176-4
ISBN 978-1-84550-176-1

10 9 8 7 6 5 4 3 2 1

Published in 2006
by
Christian Focus Publications Ltd.,
Geanies House, Fearn, Tain,
Ross-shire, IV20 1TW, Scotland
www.christianfocus.com

Cover design by Moose77.com

Printed and bound by J. H. Haynes, Sparkford

CONTENTS

1. WOMEN OF GRACE 5

2. TAMAR'S STORY...13

3. PAM'S STORY 25

4. RAHAB'S STORY 37

5. KAREN'S STORY 47

6. RUTH'S STORY...53

7. FRAN'S STORY...63

8. BATHSHEBA'S STORY 73

9. JUDY'S STORY...81

10. MARY OF NAZARETH'S STORY 91

11. NANCY'S STORY 107

12. THE SAMARITAN WOMAN'S STORY 119

13. CAMILLE'S STORY 129

14. MY STORY 141

1

WOMEN OF GRACE

I have always wanted to be a graceful girl – lady – woman. It was not to be. I am closer to the klutz category: I can stumble over nothing; my hand-to-eye coordination is poor; I knock things over easily, run into doors frequently, lose my balance standing still. Grace is not my forte.

During my freshman year of college, my parents sent me to a woman who was going to teach me to be graceful. It was a good idea; they recognized my shortcomings and tried to help. She showed me how to sit, how to walk, how to take bows on stage, and such like. I enjoyed the lessons, but I could see in the instructor's eyes the 'hopeless case' look.

Once, as an adult, I enrolled for ballet lessons at a local community college. Another good idea, but my plies left much to be desired. I admit it, I'm not graceful, but I can tell you that I am a woman full of grace; God's incredible grace, which has been showered upon me with never-ending abundance. So are you. So are we all. What does that mean? Simply that the Almighty God, Creator of heaven and earth, Ruler of the universe has shown me favor beyond belief, heaped on me kindnesses and benefits that I have not earned and do not deserve.

MERCY AND GRACE
My Webster's dictionary says that a synonym for 'grace' is 'mercy', but I beg to differ. Grace is even more than mercy. Mercy is God letting me off the hook. I deserve punishment for my sins because

I am guilty; I deserve the penalty imposed by God's law for sinners, which is death, but in great mercy, God has let me off the hook.

Because Jesus paid the price I owed for my sins through His death on Calvary, God is free to be merciful to me and not demand of me what I owe. His holiness would be violated if He simply overlooked my sins; atonement is essential. So Jesus paid the price, and now God can and does show mercy to me. God says, 'You're guilty, Mary; you deserve the full penalty of sin, but I will be merciful to you because you have accepted my Son as your Savior. Therefore, you do not have to pay the debt of your sin.'

That is mercy – and is it ever wonderful! Without mercy none of us could have a relationship with the Holy God. Without mercy none of us could avoid the debt we owe. Without mercy we are all doomed. Mercy would have been enough.

But God goes beyond mercy and gives me grace – His favor in abundance. It is as though the judge, who found me guilty and forgave my debt and showed me mercy, now comes out from behind his judge's desk, puts his arm around me, the guilty sinner, and says, 'Now that you are free from the guilt and debt of your sin, let me take you into my home, rehabilitate you, clothe you, feed you, take care of you, and make you into something worthwhile.'

Why would God (the Judge) do that? Mercy is enough. Why would God stoop to my level and show me such favor? There is only one answer: God is gracious. 'The LORD is gracious and compassionate, slow to anger and rich in love' (Ps. 145:8).

GRACEFUL VERSUS GRACE-FULL

So, while I may not naturally be very graceful, I am miraculously grace-full – full of God's grace. And while it would be nice to be both graceful and grace-full, the latter is far more important than the former. I choose grace-full, hands down. The Apostle Paul expressed his appreciation for God's grace so well:

> I thank Christ Jesus our Lord, who has given me strength, that He considered me faithful, appointing me to His service. Even though I was once a blasphemer and a persecutor and a violent man, I was shown mercy because I acted in ignorance and unbelief. The grace of our Lord was poured out on me abundantly, along with the faith and love that are in Christ Jesus (1 Tim. 1:12-14).

His testimony could be mine with slight changes of words, for the grace of our Lord was poured out on me abundantly, in spite of my failures, my past, my long side-trip while 'doing my own thing'. Because God is gracious, I am allowed to be His servant and to know His love and peace, contentment and joy. Grace – marvelous, incredible grace.

That is what this book is about – God's grace. Now, what could I possibly add to this subject that hasn't already been said much better by others more qualified and articulate? Nothing new, I'm sure. But the purpose of this book is to remind us all of grace and the role it plays in our everyday lives.

REMEMBER GRACE

You see, we are prone to forget; we are prone to take credit where none is due to us; we are prone to take for granted the grace of God. We need reminders in many forms to bring us back to the grace of God.

Christians who are focused on God's grace are compassionate, tender, thankful people, with servant attitudes. The more we think about God's grace, the less pride we have in our lives. The more we remind ourselves over and over again of what God's grace has done for us, the less we struggle with self-esteem, self-confidence, self-image.

On the days I keep in my mind my position in Christ and the blessings that are mine because of God's grace, I am a positive, productive, energetic woman. Think of what the following passage means:

And God raised us up with Christ and seated us with Him in the heavenly realms in Christ Jesus, in order that in the coming ages He might show the incomparable riches of His grace, expressed in His kindness to us in Christ Jesus (Eph. 2:6-7).

I have to admit that my mind blows a circuit when I try to imagine what it means to be 'seated with Him in the heavenly realms in Christ Jesus.' God has already seated me there. It is a done deal. That is where I am now, because God wants to show me, and the world around me, how incomparably rich His grace is in my life.

Of course, people don't look at me on a daily basis and remark, 'Look, there's Mary seated in the heavenly realms in Christ Jesus.' The world around me can't see the invisible things of God, because 'the God of this age has blinded the minds of unbelievers, so that they cannot see the light of the gospel of the glory of Christ, who is the image of God' (2 Cor. 4:4). Frankly, there are times and days when I can't see those heavenly realms very well, and I sometimes find them hard to believe myself.

So, how do I know that I am already 'seated in the heavenly realms in Christ Jesus'? It is because that is what the Word of God teaches me, and I can see the results of God's grace in my life. When I choose to, I can clearly see how rich I am because God has poured His grace on me. Not just His mercy, but also His incomparable grace.

While those around me may be blinded to the light of the Gospel, they can still see that an unworthy, unqualified, unlikely woman has found contentment, meaning, purpose and joy in a world that is restless, joyless, peace-less and seemingly meaningless. They can see how rich I am because of God's grace, even though they may not understand the full implications. Because God has chosen to shower on me the incomparable riches of His grace, I am no longer who I used to be. I am no longer chained to my poor self-image; I am no longer a prisoner of what others think or say about me; I am not limited by my past, my failures or my inadequacies, nor by my lack of education or experience. I can tell you what grace has done for me and for others. I can demonstrate the effects of being seated with Him in the heavenly realms, and I can testify that His grace is available to do for you what it has done for so many others:

> God is able to make all grace abound to you, so that in all things at all times, having all that you need, you will abound in every good work (2 Cor. 9:8).

I believe a right understanding of God's grace can deliver us from the self-focus that is so prevalent and so damaging. We are told that women's greatest common struggle is low self-esteem. I wonder if we've heard it so often that we've talked ourselves into believing it, so that it has become a self-fulfilling prophecy? Well, if it is true that our gender has a case of low self-esteem, what is the answer? Getting better jobs? Earning more money? Holding higher positions? Keeping cleaner houses? Raising perfect children? We've tried all that and it has not seemed to improve our lot.

The answer to low self-esteem is to understand what God's grace has done for us: it has seated us beside Jesus Christ in heavenly realms. That is how God sees us, and when we see ourselves that way, we become God-focused, not self-focused, rejoicing daily in His grace that truly enables us to be 'somebody'. The more we remember who we are because of grace, the less we will struggle with what we call 'low self-esteem'.

THE POWER OF GRACE

I truly believe this grace-mindedness can cure and heal, but also elevate, motivate and empower us. The Bible tells us that as we think in our hearts, so are we (Prov. 23:7, KJV), and if we think grace in our hearts, we will be grace-full. And when we are grace-full, we are joy-full and peace-full. Joy and peace and contentment are inevitable fruits of being aware of God's grace.

You see, even though many, if not most of you reading this, have received God's grace and been made new through His mercy, you may not be living grace-full lives. If not, that is because you aren't aware enough of God's grace in your life. So, instead of being grace-full, you are too often stress-full and worry-full, depressed and discouraged.

All you need to do is ask God to teach you how to be grace-full, and on a daily basis pray for grace-fullness. Sound too simple? Believe me, it is not complicated; it is simple. You and I must choose to make the focus of our thoughts and lives the grace that God has extended toward us in boundless measure.

DEMONSTRATIONS OF GRACE

How do we do that? By filling up our minds with stories of grace, with Scriptures of grace, with songs of grace, and with the truth of grace, so that we are more easily reminded of God's grace. That is why I have written this book. It is designed to help you see the reality of God's grace as it has been demonstrated in the lives of thirteen women. I'm going to tell you the stories of six women in Scripture and seven contemporary women who have been transformed by God's grace. You will see as you read these stories that these women were not and are not perfect. The seven contemporary women are still in the process of 'growing in grace'. In the process of reading these relevant stories, my prayer is that you will catch a new glimpse of grace and what it means in your life.

I know you'll remember a story better than anything else, and I want you to remember one of these stories when your days are long, your heart heavy, your body weary or you are ready to quit. I believe God will bring these stories to your mind again and again, to remind you of what God's grace has done for others and, thereby, what it has done and can do for you.

WHY THESE GRACE-FULL WOMEN?

You may wonder how I chose these particular women. Well, one day I was reading again the first chapter of Matthew. If you recall, the first sixteen verses of that chapter contain a record of the genealogy of Jesus, starting with Abraham. Genealogies were very important documents back then, particularly in the Jewish tradition. Even more than today, people's pedigrees were critical to their acceptance, their opportunities, their designated roles in life. Jewish genealogies followed very traditional guidelines – namely, a genealogy was tracked through the male family members. Usually, women's names were not included. That seems strange to my female mind. I always want to say, 'You guys couldn't have done this by yourselves!' But that is just the way it was done.

In light of that, these first sixteen verses of Matthew 1 become very interesting indeed, because they contain references to five women. When I realized that, it immediately raised some questions in my mind. As I thought about the twenty-eight generations from Abraham to Jesus, I wondered:

- Why are only five women mentioned, out of all the dozens of women who had to be involved?
- Why are any women mentioned at all? Matthew was a Jew, so he knew how genealogies were traditionally recorded.
- Why these five women?

That last question really began to intrigue me as I looked at those five women, knowing something of their stories. First, in verse three we have Tamar, the mother of Perez, one of the twin boys she gave birth to through a deceptive, incestuous relationship with her father-in-law, Judah. Why Tamar?

Then, in verse five we find Rahab referenced as the mother of Boaz. Rahab the Harlot is her familiar, infamous name. That is right, she was a harlot, and besides that, she was not even a Jew. Why Rahab?

Then in that same verse five we find Ruth, who was Rahab's daughter-in-law. Ruth married Boaz. You remember that wonderful love story of how Boaz took Ruth for his bride when she and her first mother-in-law, Naomi, were about to starve. I like Ruth a lot, but Ruth was a Moabite woman in the midst of a Jewish genealogy. Why Ruth?

In verse six another woman is mentioned: '...whose mother had been Uriah's wife.' This one really puzzled me. Why did not Matthew call Bathsheba by name? Anyone knowing anything about David knows how he killed Uriah after committing adultery with his wife, Bathsheba. It is no secret who Uriah's wife was. We all know her sad story; it is not exactly the story of a virtuous woman. Why Bathsheba?

Finally, in verse sixteen, Matthew ends his genealogy with Joseph, 'the husband of Mary, of whom was born Jesus, who is called Christ.' Here's one man who is known by the woman he married, rather than the other way around. This was certainly one female name that could not be ignored in the genealogy of Jesus. Mary was the most blessed woman who ever lived, because she was given the privilege of bringing to birth the Son of Man, God made flesh. If you're going to list any women's names in the genealogy of Jesus, Mary's has to be there. But the question I asked was: why was she chosen for this honor? She did not have the education, wealth or credentials you would expect for such a calling. Why Mary?

These questions drove me to do some research and meditation about these five women. From that came a series of messages on these five women – women of grace – and I saw how encouraging it was to women today to learn about these grace-full women. Eventually, we dramatized this message of hope, and that drama has been used across the country and internationally by many groups to encourage even more women through the stories of these women of grace.

Now I have the opportunity to tell their stories in book format, and I have added one other biblical woman, the Samaritan woman, or the 'Woman at the Well'. She is one of the nameless women in Scripture whose story has impacted the world. As I retell the circumstances of each of their lives here, it is with the prayer that we will all learn some important principles from each of them – principles that we can apply in our daily living.

TODAY'S GRACE-FULL WOMEN

One of the greatest blessings of my ministry to women is the opportunity I have to get to know many women of grace today. I have for a long time wanted to share some of these stories with others, because they have encouraged me so much. So I have chosen six very different women, each of whom, like the six biblical women, has been miraculously lifted and changed by God's grace. Some of their stories are dramatic; some are still very much 'in-progress'; some may reflect experiences you have had. But in each case they are grace-full women whom I know personally to be transformed by the power of God's grace. I have only used the first names of these women, and sometimes a fictitious name, in order to protect family members and others, but I can assure you that each of these is flesh and blood, a real woman who has been forever transformed by God's astonishing grace. They have agreed to share their sometimes private and painful stories so that others can be reminded of how deep and wide and marvelous God's grace is.

I have also included my own testimony of God's grace in my life. I never tire of telling it, because it reminds me again of where I was before Jesus took over and where I would be without Him. David, as he so often does, expresses God's grace in my life so well in Psalm 40:2-3:

> He lifted me out of the slimy pit, out of the mud and mire; he set my feet on a rock and gave me a firm place to stand. He put a new song in my mouth; a hymn of praise to our God. Many will see and fear and put their trust in the LORD.

If you feel like you are still in the mud and mire of that slimy pit, my prayer is that this book will give you a new or renewed glimpse of grace which will put a new song in your mouth that many will see and hear.

2

TAMAR'S STORY

Tamar was a victim: a victim of men, a victim of society and a victim of circumstances. She did not deserve all the bad things that happened to her. Her two husbands and her father-in-law treated her despicably. The laws and customs of her day were terribly discriminatory against her as a woman. If you want to see a real victim, look at Tamar.

TAMAR'S PREDICAMENT

You'll find her story in Genesis 38. It is a sordid story. The Bible never whitewashes people or events, so be prepared for the raw truth when you read this chapter. (If you have not read it recently, it would be a good idea to stop here and do just that. It is only thirty verses, and a very fast read!)

As I write this book, I am in the midst of teaching the Book of Genesis to my Sunday Bible class, so I have been immersed in the background that led up to Tamar's story. Jacob had twelve sons who eventually became heads of the twelve tribes of Israel. Jacob's fourth son was Judah, and Tamar married Judah's son, Er, one of Jacob's grandsons.

Tamar had married into a very prestigious family. Prestigious, yes; righteous, no. Today we would say that Tamar married into a very dysfunctional family. Ten of Jacob's sons had already left a trail of blood behind them; they were treacherous, murderous liars, without natural affection, scheming and deceptive. These were the boys who viciously plotted and carried out a deceptive attack on their neighbors, murdering all the men, and carrying off all their wealth and their women and children (Gen. 34). These were the same guys who first planned to kill their innocent brother, Joseph, but decided instead to sell him as a slave and then tell their father he had been killed.

So, when Judah picked Tamar to be Er's wife, he did her no big favor. It would have been best for Tamar to say, 'Thanks, but no thanks,' but she had no choice. She had to marry the man chosen for her by her family. She was a victim of the system.

Sadly, it did not take long for her to see how victimized she was. Er was so wicked that before she even had a chance to establish a home with children by Er, God put him to death. We aren't told explicitly what wicked acts earned him this judgment, but we have to believe they were bad. God allowed his uncles to live even though they committed wicked acts, but Er was just more than God chose to tolerate. So, not long after her wedding, Tamar became a childless widow.

TAMAR'S DISGRACE

It is difficult for us to relate to Tamar's position in her society because it was so different from society today. For any married woman to be childless was a disgrace. Women were always blamed for infertility, and a man had a right to abandon his wife if she were childless, or at least take another wife to bear children. Having a male heir to carry on the family name was of paramount importance to men, and whatever it took to accomplish that end was justifiable.

Keep in mind that this was not God's way, but man's way — and, as is always true, it got them into heaps of trouble. Think of Abraham and Hagar and Ishmael; think of Jacob's liaisons with the handmaids of Leah and Rachel. The world today is still reeling from the aftermath of this obsession to have a man-child to carry on the family name.

In order to make certain that every man had an heir to perpetuate his family line, custom dictated that if a man died before bearing a son, his brother or brothers were obligated to marry the widow for the purpose of allowing her to bear a son for the dead husband. While she would bear the brother's child, that child would be legally accepted as her dead husband's son, to carry on his name. That boy would take the name and the inheritance of the dead brother. That sure seems strange to us, but this is a custom still practiced in some cultures in Africa, and probably elsewhere as well.

TAMAR'S SECOND CHANCE

So, the widow Tamar again was without any say in the matter – she now had to marry Er's brother, Onan. Onan really had no choice either; his father commanded him to fulfill his duty to Tamar to produce offspring for his brother. Onan was not wild about the idea; not that he minded having sex with Tamar, but he knew that the son she would bear from their union would not legally be his son, but Er's heir. Because Er had been the firstborn, a son born to Tamar would receive the family inheritance, the family money, the family power. So Onan decided to sabotage the plan. Every time he had sex with Tamar, he would purposely avoid impregnating her by 'spilling his semen on the ground,' as Genesis 38 vividly tells us. This certainly required some strong self-discipline on his part, which demonstrates how determined he was not to allow Tamar to have Er's son.

Onan thought he could get away with this deception. After all, who would know that he had spilled his semen on the ground? Everybody else in the family saw that he had married Tamar, as required, and knew that he went in to her tent on a regular basis to have sex. If Tamar did not get pregnant and bear a son for Er, no one would believe it was Onan's fault. They would blame it on Tamar. In the dark of night and the privacy of that tent, Onan felt sure he could get away with his plan.

But God knew what Onan was up to. He saw the wickedness and greed of his heart, and so He chose to bring swift judgment on Onan by putting him to death, just as He had done with Er.

In 1 Corinthians 4:5 we read: 'Therefore judge nothing before the appointed time; wait till the Lord comes. He will bring to light what is hidden in darkness and will expose the motives of men's hearts.' Certainly Onan is proof of how God exposes evil schemes hatched in darkness.

TAMAR'S DILEMMA

Put yourself in Tamar's shoes about now. She wants to have a child; without a child she is truly a nobody in that culture. Her father-in-law, Judah, is bound by custom and tradition to take care of her and to help her bear a child for his son, Er. If Tamar does not bear a child, she will not only be disgraced, but her means of support throughout her entire life will be in jeopardy. Judah would be obligated to her if she bore his grandchild, but if not, he could throw her out without a second thought if he chose to. Tamar is well aware that her whole future hinges on her ability to bear a son for Er, her dead, wicked husband.

For that reason, Tamar was most likely glad to entertain Onan for the purpose of becoming pregnant; he was her only hope. While we don't know how often Onan had sex with Tamar and spilled his semen, we can tell from Genesis 38:9 that it was much more than once. The verse says, 'so whenever he lay with his brother's wife, he spilled his semen on the ground,' indicating repeated encounters.

Surely Tamar knew what Onan was doing; she was in that dark tent with him, and he couldn't hide his deceptive intentions from her. What should she do? I wonder if she had a talk with Onan about it. I wonder if they talked at all, or if he simply performed his duty as dictated by his father, without any personal concern for Tamar whatsoever. Was she just a non-person to him, someone he could use and abuse at will?

Could Tamar have gone to Judah and reported Onan's deceptive behavior? Would Judah have believed her? Did she try to make Onan do the right thing? We don't know the answers to those questions; the details are not included in Genesis 38. But Tamar was a normal woman like you and me, so I'm sure she was aware of what was being done to her by this second wicked man, Onan.

TAMAR'S DESPERATE CONDITION

My guess is that Tamar was alone in this ordeal. She likely had no one to talk to, no one to take her side, no one to intervene on her behalf. She was trapped in this dysfunctional family, doomed to be a victim of their wickedness. Day after day, week after week, as she considered her plight, my guess is that Tamar became a bit paranoid and obsessive about having a baby. A baby would secure her position in the family; a baby would ensure that she would get her 'social security' payments until the end of her life; a baby was essential to her happiness, prosperity, livelihood and security. Tamar had to have a baby.

After God killed Onan, Tamar was left with just one option – Judah's last son, Shelah. He was still young, so Judah instructed Tamar to go live with her father until Shelah 'grew up' and could then do for Tamar what Onan was supposed to do – give her a son for his brother, Er.

Every time I imagine what was going through Tamar's mind about this time, I find anger and frustration welling up inside me. Tamar, keep in mind, was innocent in all this mess. She did nothing wrong. But because of Judah's two wicked sons, she was childless – the worst thing in the world for a woman to be. It would have been easier to be unmarried than to be married and childless. As an unmarried woman, her father would have been obligated to continue to care for her, but as a childless widow, she was totally at the mercy of her father-in-law's whims. And Judah certainly did not behave admirably toward her. He deceived her by telling her she could marry Shelah when he was older, when in reality he was thinking, 'I don't want Tamar to marry Shelah. He may die too, just like his brothers.'

TAMAR'S LONG WAIT
So, Tamar the victim went back to her father's house to bide the time until Judah would give her Shelah. She was in a lose-lose situation, powerless to do anything. She was not allowed to marry anyone else, and waiting for Shelah to reach a suitable age was certainly not promising. Her life was put on hold for who knows how long, and all because she had been forced to marry into a wicked, dysfunctional family. Tamar was victimized, no doubt about it.

She was trapped in this unenviable position for a long time. Genesis 38:12 tells us that 'after a long time' Judah's wife died. And during all this 'long time,' Tamar was living with her father, waiting for Judah to fulfill his promise to her so that she could have a child. She was a woman without a country – so to speak. She was not really a part of her father's family, and Judah did not want her around his family.

TAMAR'S PLAN
During this time Tamar had plenty of opportunity to consider her predicament. My guess is that she had plenty of time to become bitter, angry, vindictive and obsessive. The more she thought about it, the more she saw her only hope was somehow, some way, to bear a son to Judah, thus forcing him to give her the rightful place she

deserved in his family. She was determined not to let these men victimize her any longer. It was time to take action.

My heart and sympathy go out to Tamar. I can see myself doing exactly what she did – coming up with my own plan to get what I wanted, what I deserved, what I had coming to me. After all, none of this was Tamar's fault, and she did not intend to have her life ruined by these evil, heartless men.

She devised a plan to pose as a prostitute and deceive her widowed father-in-law into having sex with her. Here it helps to understand the background a bit. Being a Canaanite, Tamar was from a culture where promiscuity and prostitution were ways of life. In fact, the profession of temple prostitute was considered respectable. Living as she had been in Judah's wicked household, she might never have really learned God's view of these practices. So, her plan of posing as a prostitute and entrapping her hapless father-in-law most likely did not seem evil to her mind. (Of course, that doesn't mean it was not evil; it just helps to understand how she might have been thinking.)

I often wonder why she went after Judah rather than Shelah. She must have deliberately chosen Judah for some reason. Maybe it was simply opportunity – Judah was looking for a prostitute and Shelah may not have been. It might have been that Shelah was not accessible to her or still just not old enough. Or perhaps she decided that if she entrapped Judah himself and was bearing his baby, she would have the strongest leverage in this situation to accomplish her end. We don't know her reason, but she had plenty of time to consider all her options, and she must have felt entrapping Judah offered her the best potential. She waited for the right time, and then when she heard that Judah was going to a sheep shearing, she knew that this was probably her best opportunity.

Sheep-shearing time, for the pagan religions of that day, was a good excuse for 'boys to be boys.' After the sheep were sheared, the men of Judah usually held a festival, which included all kinds of corrupt and disgraceful activities. Engaging a harlot was one of the more common of these festival pursuits for many men.

JUDAH'S DOWNFALL

Note that Judah attends the festivities with his friend, Hirah. Hirah is not of the same religion as Judah. He is an Adullamite, from a pagan nation and religion, yet he is Judah's good friend. Hirah is not a good influence on Judah. Notice that Judah goes to his pagan festivities, rather than leading Hirah to worship the true God.

Judah had left his family and friends of his faith, and followed Hirah to a place where he should not have been – a pagan festival. And in that wrong place, he was exposed to a harlot by the road who offered him her services. It was not difficult for him to rationalize his behavior at this point. He was a widower, so he was not betraying his wife. He needed sexual companionship; it was just a normal need that must be met. Everybody was doing it. No one would know. What harm could it do? Had Judah stopped to give his behavior a second thought, can't you hear him rationalizing it this way?

Keep in mind that Judah had married a Canaanite woman who was not of his faith, and this was in direct opposition to God's instructions. Now that his wife was dead, he could easily fall into the 'poor me' syndrome in order to justify the evil act he decided to do. 'Poor me – my wife is dead and I have no one to sleep with me at night. Poor me – my two oldest sons died suddenly and I have had a hard life. Poor me – I could lose my other son if he marries Tamar. Oh, poor me – I deserve a break today!'

I can imagine Judah thinking this way because I have found myself thinking similarly on many occasions. Because I think I have been particularly hard-working or faithful or 'put upon,' or inconvenienced for the sake of the Lord, I can start to think that I have earned credits which let me off the hook in other areas. It is a very deceptive line of thinking which can quickly take you down the wrong path. It is easy to forget that God's principles are there for my good, not to torture me.

Judah knew God would not approve of prostitution, but at that moment in time, seeing the woman accessible to him, he might have decided he had a right to take advantage of this opportunity because of all his other trials and tribulations, and his own imagined, overwhelming physical needs which could be satisfied in no other way, so he thought.

What Judah forgot to compute as he made this decision were the consequences. As I have said so often, you can choose your sin but you can't choose its consequences. Judah made wrong choices all along the way that eventually brought him to this place of temptation. It did not just happen. He married the wrong woman;

he treated his daughter-in-law wrongly; he went to the wrong place with the wrong friend. Had he walked the straight-and-narrow road at any of these junctures in his past, he would not have been there at that sheep-shearing festival.

Can you look back over your life and see a trail of bad decisions that have brought you to a difficult place? How often we wish we could go back and change some of our decisions to avoid the consequences that have come with them! Be encouraged to know that while you may have to suffer through some of the consequences of those wrong choices and decisions, God can take any mess you've made and turn it into something good and useful. That is what this book is all about!

TAMAR'S SUCCESS

You can tell from Tamar's plan that she was a patient and intelligent woman. She came up with a way to entice and entrap Judah. She waited until the time was right, and she executed her plan flawlessly. What she did was to blackmail Judah. By keeping Judah's seal and cord, and also his staff, Tamar had undeniable proof that she had slept with Judah. The fact that Judah showed no reluctance to leave those highly distinguishable things with her indicates he was never the least bit suspicious of who she was, or why she asked for such a pledge of his commitment to give her a goat for her services.

In case you are wondering why he did not recognize her when they were alone, prostitutes in those days kept a black veil over their faces at all times to avoid recognition. So nothing seemed unusual to Judah. It would seem that these immoral encounters were without tenderness or caring, as would undoubtedly be the case today in similar situations. For Judah, it was simply a way to have his needs met without any personal involvement. He got what he wanted and left quickly, I would guess.

Judah tried to send her the goat he promised by way of his friend, Hirah, but he could not find this unknown prostitute. Hirah asked around: 'Where's the prostitute that was beside the road?' Everybody declared there was no such prostitute in that place. Another indication of Tamar's astute execution of this smart plan.

When Judah learned that the goat could not be delivered, and therefore his possessions could not be returned, he said, 'Let her keep what she has, or we will become a laughing- stock. After all, I did send her this young goat, but you did not find her' (Gen. 38:23). In other words, if he kept looking for her and asking about her whereabouts, the people of the area would start to make fun of him. So he said, 'let it go – let her have the staff and seal.'

Now, I have wondered what value that staff and seal would have had for anyone except Judah. Staffs were individually carved and designed for people, and the richer you were, the more ornate your staff would be. It was a way of advertising your status and riches. The seal was used to verify a person's identity; it too would be unique to Judah and used solely by him to put his 'mark of approval' on documents, etc. My guess is that these things had value, were expensive, and Judah really wanted them back. If they had no value to Judah, Tamar would not have asked for them as a pledge.

Yet, even though he wanted them back, he decided to forego them rather than 'become a laughing-stock' (Gen. 38:23). If Judah had continued to search for the unknown prostitute, it would have been like advertising the stupidity of his arrangement and how easily he was duped and fooled. It would also have become known to more and more people that he had slept with a prostitute. Maybe Judah was embarrassed and ashamed of that act.

Of course, Tamar had to wait again to see if her plan had succeeded. Success, in her mind, was to become pregnant. Three months later it became obvious that indeed Tamar was pregnant and word spread to Judah.

What happened at this point is a good example of a double standard. Judah threatened to have her burned to death, which – believe it or not – was his legal right as her father-in-law. Tamar could be killed for her promiscuous behavior. Of course, once pregnant she could not conceal her sin and so Judah ordered her to be burned, even though he had been guilty of promiscuity himself. In that culture it was standard procedure to take it out on the woman.

Tamar, of course, knew exactly what would happen, and she was ready. She had requested from Judah tokens that could never be discredited or denied. He could not accuse her of manufacturing this story, and to his credit, he admitted his involvement. He did not try to get out of his responsibility, and treated Tamar appropriately from that point. He even conceded that Tamar was more righteous than he was and admitted he had withheld what was rightfully hers – marriage to Shelah, his youngest son.

Note that Judah says she was more righteous than he was, which was not the same as saying she had a righteous and God-blessed plan. Perhaps he should more accurately have said that her plan was less wrong or less evil than his. They were both in the deception business. He was trying to deceive Tamar by promising her Shelah but never intending to fulfill his promise. Tamar deceived him through a disguise and a carefully thought-out plan. It is difficult to find anything righteous about deception of any kind, but a case could be made that Tamar's motives were less selfish and more justifiable than Judah's.

Tamar succeeded in her plan. She gave birth to not just one child, but to twin boys from this liaison with Judah. Sweet success, wouldn't you say?

TAMAR'S DISGRACE

Yes, her plan succeeded in achieving her goals; but by taking matters into her own hands, she soiled her reputation and engraved this ugly episode in the book of Genesis for all to read for thousands of years. She is not remembered as a woman of virtue or righteousness. Even the fact that she was a victim and treated badly does not erase the sour taste that this story leaves behind. Though she had her sons, she most likely never had a husband again. Judah never touched her again or offered to marry her, although he probably could have, if he had so desired, and it is highly doubtful that he gave Shelah to her since she already had her baby boys. The remainder of her days might have been very lonely, though Judah most likely took care of her and the boys for the rest of their lives.

God sometimes allows us to succeed in our wrong plans, because He has given us free will, and that means we can make wrong choices. But when we succeed through our own manipulation, we always pay the price. Yet I am convinced that God chose Tamar to be the grandmother – many times removed – of our Lord Jesus Christ, and that He would have worked this out for her in His way, at His time, had she been willing to trust Him. Tamar was victimized in spite of her obedience and innocence. God would have given her an honorable way to become the mother of Perez, if she could have but trusted Him.

Many times in Scripture we see how God works His will even though the people involved try to manipulate things their way. Look at Abraham and Sarah and the sad results of Sarah's way of working God's will out for their lives. We live today with the animosity and enmity that began with the birth of Ishmael to Hagar, Sarah's maid. It was Sarah's way to fulfill God's plan, but if she had just waited for God's plan, that whole terrible saga would never have occurred.

When we rush ahead of God and try to manipulate people and circumstances to achieve even good and worthy objectives, we may not necessarily thwart God's purpose, but we will deprive ourselves of the joy of watching God do it for us, and the peace that comes from waiting for God. We do ourselves great harm when we run ahead of God and try to do His work for Him.

TAMAR'S REDEMPTION

Yes, Tamar was a victim, and this pushed her to take action rather than leaving things in God's hands. She has left behind a picture of a woman who was obsessed, desperate and willing to do anything to get what she believed to be her right. Her success is tainted forever, and yet God was still able to take her son, Perez, and make him a forefather of King David and an ancestor of Jesus Christ. Tamar's name is in Matthew 1 as the mother of Perez. God redeemed her and used the good from her life in a miraculous way. That is grace, and it demonstrates the depth to which God's grace can reach – even to a Canaanite woman who posed as a prostitute in order to deceive her father-in-law and bear his sons. God's grace is that deep and that wide.

FROM VICTIM TO VICTORY

Perhaps you've been victimized too. Did your parents abuse you? Have you been robbed of your health or abilities by birth defects or an accident? Are you in an abusive marriage? Have you lost your job unfairly? I suppose most of us could come up with some description of ourselves as a victim.

The good news of Tamar's story is that victims can do more than just survive. Victims can be redeemed! Victims can become victorious! That is because no one is beyond the astonishing grace of God. There is no mess so big, no disgrace so great, no mistake so disastrous that God can't make something good out of it. If there is a place in God's plan for Tamar, in spite of the ugliness of her predicament, you can be confident that the same God who delivered her has good plans for you as well.

Paul wrote, 'By the grace of God I am what I am, and His grace to me was not without effect' (1 Cor. 15:10). The grace God extended to Tamar was not without effect. She was placed in the lineage of Jesus Christ, her name forever inscribed in that most prestigious of all genealogies. If you are in the victim category right now, God is extending grace to you. There is grace all around you, waiting for you to respond. If you are saying, 'I don't see any grace in my life,' then maybe it is because you haven't yet been willing to give up your role as the victim.

I would urge you to give God permission to exchange your present state of victimization for His glorious and victorious grace. Tell Him that you are willing to give up your right to feel sorry for yourself and to stop wallowing in your victimization. You can go from victim to victory today, right now, if you will make that commitment to God by faith. He provides the grace; you must accept it. Then you too can say, 'By the grace of God, I am what I am!'

Let me tell you about a friend of mine who is further proof that God still redeems the lives of victims.

3

PAM'S STORY

Pam was a victim. Like Tamar, she was a victim of her culture, her dysfunctional family, her society and her own manipulative maneuvering.

Of course, victims can be beautiful and Pam certainly is. With her flawless complexion, her beautiful face and a smile that never quits, she makes a striking impression. She is a black woman who looks many years younger than she is, but the years of her life have been full of incredible ups and downs, joy and pain, plenty and nothing.

A CHILDHOOD IN TWO WORLDS

Pam was born in the deep South, the fifth child of her mother. Her father never married her mother, which cast a stigma over Pam's life from day one. While it was many years before she understood what the word illegitimate meant, by the time she could talk and walk she was aware of the whispering that went on behind her back about 'that little girl' who had been born out of wedlock. Rejection, with all its pain, penetrated her heart at a very early age.

Unlike many others in similar situations, her father did not abandon her; in fact, he had great concern for her and made sure she was well cared for. He did not take care of her mother, however, and Pam grew up in this very unnatural environment of plenty and poverty. She loved both her father and mother, but was pulled between their two worlds.

Pam learned quickly that she was treated much better when she visited her dad; people were warm and friendly, and accepted her as one of them. Her father's money and prestige paved the way for her, so she enjoyed her father's world very much. Also, her father was generous in his financial support of her. For a young girl over forty years ago, she had big money, and it meant that Pam could have the clothes she needed and wanted, and plenty of food to eat. She was able to avoid the feeling of being poor even though she lived in her mother's home.

At home with her mother, however, life was much more difficult. Her mother worked in the fields to earn meager daily wages and her home was very poor. Her father gave her financial security, yet her mother provided emotional security. Her mother's arms provided a place of retreat for Pam during those childhood days. Often she cried in her mother's arms about the way people treated her, trying to understand what she had done to deserve this abuse. Her mother gave her sympathy and love, but she could give Pam no explanations. In a sense, the sins of the mother were being visited upon the daughter, and while Pam's mother hurt with her, she could not explain or assuage the rejection and hurt in her little girl's heart.

Daily life for Pam was a continual contradiction of messages from two different worlds. The world around her was fickle, sometimes showing approval and acceptance, but other times dishing out rejection and condemnation.

Death's Ugly Face

As if all this were not enough for a young girl, her world was suddenly shattered when her dad died. Pam was almost ten years old, and she well remembers the terror she felt at his funeral. Fearful of viewing his body, she ran out of the church during the service and tried to escape the horror of death. She went through the confusion, the anger and the false guilt that is common when a young child loses a parent. How could he leave her? He was her financial security. His world offered her hope and acceptance. His sudden death was devastating in every way imaginable.

This put an abrupt end to the pleasant world Pam had come to enjoy. Though her father never married anyone, he had lived with a woman who managed to confiscate all his papers and, with the help of a lawyer, took all that Pam's father had accumulated. Pam should have inherited money from her father's estate to assure her a comfortable life, an education and a secure financial underpinning, but these were stolen from her by this unethical, greedy woman and her lawyer.

Pam's family realized what had happened, and they tried to intervene on her behalf. But because they were seriously threatened by this woman's lawyer, and they felt their lives were in danger, they had to abandon their pursuit of Pam's inheritance.

A ten-year old could not comprehend the full extent of this turn of events, but Pam's daily life immediately reflected these changes. The weekly allowance stopped; the special gifts stopped. There were no more excursions into the world of the well-to-do. Those intermittent times when she felt special ended with her father's death.

Abruptly, life changed. From a fairly comfortable life with enough money for life's necessities and even some luxuries, Pam's world became one of total poverty. She had to go to work in the fields with her mother to pay her own way. At the weekends during school months, and in the hot months of summer vacation, she had to work in the cotton fields. She was paid $5 a day in the springtime, when she was chopping cotton – cleaning the weeds from around the young cotton plants. In the fall harvest-time, she earned $5 for each 100 pounds of picked cotton.

She carried a sack that would hold about twenty-five pounds of cotton, and the best she would be able to do in a day's work would be four sacks full – or 100 pounds – $5 per day. She remembers looking down those long rows of cotton and wondering if she would ever make it to the end of that long row. Her mother would encourage her not to give up. It was better than nothing, she would say, and in those cotton fields Pam learned the hard lessons of surviving.

As she worked alongside her mother, she would pour her heart out again and again. 'Mama, why didn't daddy leave us some money? Didn't he love me? What is going to happen to me without my daddy?' Often she would complain about the hard work and ask why she had to do such work when other girls her age did not have to. Her mother had no answers. All she could do was open up her loving arms and hold Pam tight, trying to squeeze away the pain and hurt that bombarded her. The refuge she found with her mother was the only thing that made life bearable for Pam.

If her father's death was a blow to her, it was nothing compared to her dismay when, two years later, her mother was found dead.

The one person who had been her solid rock through her twelve years was suddenly gone. Her mother's love, which had made life manageable, was stolen by the monster death, and once again Pam faced devastation.

The details of her mother's death are hazy in Pam's mind; undoubtedly she blocked some of it out to avoid the pain. She remembers the funeral and the terror she felt when she saw her mother's casket. During the memorial service, she again ran out of the church.

A MOVE TO CHICAGO

Now the label of 'orphan' was added to 'illegitimate', and the anger and confusion Pam felt was almost more than she could stand. Although her grandmother took her in at the time of her mother's death, it was only a temporary arrangement.

When her extended family came from Chicago for her mother's funeral, they began to discuss Pam's future. They sent her out of the room for these discussions, but she listened through the door. She felt as if she were lost on some uncharted sea, with no control over what would happen to her. Finally, family members made a decision to take Pam to Chicago to live with her half-brother. He was more than twenty years older than Pam, and he really cared about what happened to her, so he was very much in favor of taking her into his home.

Moving from the only home and family she had ever known in a Southern town to a city like Chicago was a major culture shock for Pam. She was overwhelmed, but her survival instincts, learned in the cotton fields, kept her going.

Once she moved to Chicago, however, her half-brother's home situation deteriorated quickly, and he could no longer keep her with him. On a cold January evening, without any explanation or preparation, Pam found herself being taken to live with her grand-uncle in another part of Chicago, a man she barely knew. She longed for the familiar friends and family she had left down South. She missed her mother and grandmother. Loneliness and fear accompanied her as she moved into her uncle's home.

So, before she was thirteen years old, Pam had endured more changes and trauma, rejection, loss and confusion than most of us know in a lifetime. How much can anyone take without breaking, especially a 12-year-old girl?

Her grand-uncle eventually adopted Pam, and perhaps the family thought his home was a good place for her, because he was a very religious person. What they did not know was that he was also harsh and cold, and Pam found herself being abused by this man who was supposed to take care of her. True, he read his Bible a lot and went to church regularly, but he never spoke a kind word to her or showed her any love or compassion. She felt that she must have sinned very badly to have such a terrible life, and like many abused children, she assumed she was the guilty party and blamed herself for her problems.

RUNNING AWAY

For four years, Pam suffered in her uncle's home. The abuse became a part of her everyday experience, and those were some of the hardest years of her very young life. It was verbal abuse – often being told she was worthless and illegitimate. It was emotional abuse – withholding any signs of love or understanding from this young teenage girl. And at times, her uncle's behavior bordered on sexual abuse as well.

At the age of sixteen Pam began to think about how she could escape from the hell of living with her grand-uncle. She had no money, no safe place to run to. There was no family close by to help her. One weekend night, after a particularly angry and hurtful exchange with her grand-uncle, she simply walked out of the house and slept in the hallway of a building. The next day, when no one was around, she went back, gathered her few things, and moved out for good. She found a room in a run-down boarding house and kept her location hidden from her grand-uncle. She had a job, which paid for her room and some food.

Pam frequently stopped at one particular restaurant near her boarding house for a meal and a Coke. An older man watched her for a few days, and Pam is convinced that one evening he drugged her Coke. She remembers becoming very groggy while in the restaurant, and her next memories are of waking up in a hotel room with this stranger. He kept her there for three days, continuing to sedate her and rape her. On the third day, a maid came in to clean the room, and Pam crawled out of the room on hands and knees. She managed to get on her feet and find her way back to her boarding house, where she filled the tub with water and tried to wash away the filth and shame of that experience. She was too frightened to go to the police because, after all, she was a runaway, and she did not want to go back to her uncle's house. So she never reported the crime.

The shame of this experience overshadowed everything. Who could she run to? Who would believe her? Now, in addition to being an illegitimate orphan, she was a rape victim. She tried to put it out of her mind, but soon she was faced with the reality of a venereal disease caused by the rape. She had no choice but to seek medical help at a free clinic on Chicago's South Side. The treatment she received for the disease was painful and humiliating. Pam's feelings of loneliness and rejection intensified.

All of this caused Pam so much pain that she began to build a wall around her feelings through drug use. She knew it was addictive and harmful, but by this point she did not care. She had to find some way to deaden the shame, anger and confusion that life had heaped on her. Amazingly, she managed to maintain a job during this time, which allowed her to have a place to live. The fact that she was able to function adequately on her job was a testimony to her survival skills, which by this time had been highly honed. During her free time, she stayed high on drugs to block out the memories of her dreadful past.

MOTHERHOOD AND MARRIAGE

Having lost the love and security of her mother and father, and having endured the abuse of her grand-uncle, Pam had a deep need to be loved and accepted by someone – anyone. It is not surprising that she allowed herself to be taken in by men who wanted only a physical relationship. At the age of eighteen she became pregnant and gave birth to a girl. The lifestyle that had brought her so much pain and destruction – being born as an illegitimate child – now became her legacy to her baby daughter. It was the last thing that she wanted to happen.

Now Pam was faced with the reality of having to support her baby by herself. Though she desperately wanted to be a good mom, she had little parenting knowledge or training. For three years she did the best she could, trying to keep her daughter fed, clothed and cared for while she continued to work. It was a wonderful blessing when she found a lady who became like a godmother to her daughter, caring for her while Pam worked.

Pam felt especially fortunate when she met the 'man of her dreams,' and married him when her daughter was four years old. Since Pam was indeed a beautiful young woman, it is easy to understand how she attracted this man's attention. He not only loved her, but was willing to adopt her daughter and make her his as well. For the first time Pam could see some light at the end of her tunnel. She thought that now she had everything she ever wanted: a good husband with a good job; a good job for herself; a nice home; a father for her daughter. She was no longer the illegitimate little orphan girl. Life was finally good.

For seven years, this good life held up for Pam and her family. She was delighted when she became pregnant with her second child. The beautiful boy she gave birth to was surely just another blessing for Pam's now perfect world.

ALONE AGAIN

Yes, it was a perfect world for Pam until, shortly after their son's birth, her husband decided that he no longer wanted the responsibility of a family. Abruptly, Pam was again left to fend for herself, but now she had a little girl and an infant son. Devastated by the rejection as well as the responsibility she faced, she turned again to drugs to find relief from the pain that racked her body and mind.

As the years went by, she continued to use drugs as her escape route, trying to hide it from her children. One year led into another, her daughter started school, and then her son. She held her good job and kept them together, but it was never easy, and there was little happiness in her life. There were a series of men who came and went, as she occasionally reached out for love and security, but those relationships were always dead ends.

A WAKE-UP CALL

Pam's life rocked along in this mode, fairly aimless and somewhat deadened through the drugs, until the day she came home from work early to find her 12-year-old daughter locked in an elevator with an older boy. He had persuaded her that this would be an exciting and fulfilling experience for her, and being an impressionable girl on the verge of her teen years, she found it difficult to refuse. He knew how to stop the elevator in their building mid-floor, and when Pam arrived home that day, she could hear their voices coming from the stopped elevator. Instantly, she realized what was happening and called security.

Pam's whole life seemed to fall apart as she opened that elevator door that afternoon, surprising her daughter and the boy. But Pam was more than surprised – she was crushed. This was the bottom of the pit, as far as Pam was concerned. In that defining moment, Pam's life flashed before her eyes. Instinctively and instantaneously, she realized that she had to get a grip on her life. She had lost her home, her marriage, and now she risked losing her daughter.

Desperate, and knowing that something had to change in her life, Pam fell on her knees that night and asked God – if there was a God there at all – to help her. For the first time since she was very young, Pam began to think about God. And for the first time, she felt the beginnings of a desire to know God and to have His direction in her life. She had tried so hard to give her children all the material things they wanted, thinking this would make them happy. She had tried to make up to them what she had missed in her own childhood. But she did not understand that to be a good mom, she had to be there with them. Simply providing shelter and material things was not enough. She had ignored the whole spiritual side of life, and now she began to realize how desperately she and her children needed God.

A DIVINE CALL

In the midst of this alarming situation, a call came from Pam's half-sister in California. She had not seen her since Pam was nine years old, but out of the blue she invited Pam to move to California with her. Having just prayed for God to help her, Pam figured this was God's answer. So she gave up her good job, loaded up her few belongings, and headed west with her children.

Her sister was a believer in the Lord Jesus Christ, and Pam noticed that her radio was tuned to a Christian station regularly. Pam began to listen to all the programs on that station – every night and every morning. One particular night, the message really penetrated her heart. The preacher's text was Isaiah 1:18:

'Come now, let us reason together,' says the LORD. 'Though your sins are like scarlet they shall be as white as snow; though they are red as crimson, they shall be like wool.'

The preacher spoke right to Pam's heart as he pointed out that God didn't have to reason with the sinful people of Israel; He could have destroyed them with good cause. But He chose to reason with them because He was a God of compassion.

That was news to Pam. She listened intently as the speaker expounded on this good and gracious God, who loved her and wanted to make her sins white as snow. God was loving and kind – what a wonderful revelation this was to a girl whose only introduction to God (in the house of her grand-uncle) had left her with the idea that God was harsh and cold, if indeed He existed at all!

On that October day in 1981, she did what the preacher on the radio suggested – she asked the Lord into her life. Immediately, it felt to Pam as if a huge weight had been lifted from her. For the first time in a long time, she faced the day sober. No drugs. No alcohol. Just Jesus. And it was a high greater than any she had ever experienced.

A DIVINE HEALING

Her life began to make a turnaround. To help her put her past behind her, the Lord allowed her to face every aspect of her past as though she were watching a movie. She had tried so long to bury her past, but now each tragedy came back to life. Like a child, she responded by asking questions, reading Scripture, meditating and praying to find answers. As this ongoing movie played before her mind's eye, the Lord gently showed her how He had rescued her out of each situation. He had been there all along, though she never knew it.

She no longer looked for someone to blame. She no longer had to hide the past. She no longer needed to drown her anger and pain in drugs and alcohol. She was finally free – free to be the woman God had made her to be. She began to get to know Jesus, and in the process, she got to know herself and realized how much God loved her and had always taken care of her. Her self-worth returned, based on her value to Jesus Christ. Contentment finally entered her mind and life.

ANOTHER CHANGE, ANOTHER JOURNEY

Having found the Lord in California and having the encouragement of her Christian sister, Pam naturally assumed that her life would now settle into the California landscape. But in spite of much effort, she could not find work in California. Soon her resources were drained, and she had no option but to return to Chicago. It was hard for her to understand why God was forcing her back to Chicago. She brooded for several weeks after her return, avoiding all her friends and family, but now, with the Holy Spirit residing in her, she had the blessed presence of God with her at all times, and soon that 'still small voice' said to her, 'It is time.' Pam knew exactly what that meant – the Lord was telling her to come out of her pity party and look for a church home. Since she had listened to 'Songs in the Night' on the radio while she was in California, she was familiar with the name of Moody Church where that program originates. She decided to try that church.

That is when our paths crossed and she started coming to my home for a weekly Bible study. Her faith grew like a weed as she gobbled up the truth of God's Word for her hungry soul and mind. God blessed her even further by giving her a job in the church office, and she was promoted to the highest position she could attain in that situation. From her life on the street and on drugs, she was now surrounded with Christian friends and a Christian environment, which gave her a warm cocoon for herself and her children, now ages six and thirteen. Surely now she had found the perfect spot to settle in.

MORE HARD LESSONS

Pam began to understand that she was going to have to deal with some of the consequences of her past life as she watched her teenage daughter begin to rebel against her mother's faith and turn against the things of the Lord. She was being greatly influenced by some of the family members who lived nearby, so Pam decided to move to a near Chicago suburb, away from those bad influences.

However, her world began to fall apart again. How many times would this happen? In addition to her daughter's rebellious lifestyle, which Pam could not change no matter how hard she tried, her son began to show signs of rebellion. Then her sister in California died suddenly, as well as the sister in Chicago with whom she had lived, and she lost her job at the church. Everything was upside down again.

On top of all that, she turned forty, which she found very traumatic. Her life was passing by and it seemed to be going downhill – again. This was so difficult for her to understand because now she was a Christian. Now she was a good mother. Now she was obeying the Lord and doing everything the way she was supposed to. Why did God let these bad things happen to her now? Hadn't she suffered enough?

IN THE DESERT

She felt as if she was in a spiritual desert, and she really didn't have the desire to pursue the things of God anymore. But through this struggle, many friends prayed and stuck by Pam, showering her with support and love. In the midst of the desert experience, one passage got through to her:

> 'For I know the plans I have for you,' declares the LORD, 'plans to prosper you and not to harm you, plans to give you hope and a future' (Jer. 29:11).

Throughout the desert months and years, even when she had no idea what God was doing, she clung to the hope of this Scripture. Looking back Pam now realizes that God wanted to get her out of her 'holy huddle' life. That wasn't what she wanted, but God was preparing her for a life of outreach.

AN OASIS IN THE DESERT

In the midst of all this, a good friend read a brochure from DePaul University about a new study for adults and encouraged her to enroll and finish her education. She could not imagine how she could navigate the studies required in a large university; it looked like mission impossible to her.

Again God gave her a passage to hang on to: 'No eye has seen, no ear has heard, no mind has conceived what God has prepared for those who love Him' (1 Cor.2:9).

So her life as a student began, and it was not easy to keep going while holding down a job; but she never gave up.

AN ONGOING JOURNEY

In June of 1995 she graduated from DePaul, walking that aisle with friends and family cheering her on. She again had a very good job at management level. She got her driver's license for the first time, and even contemplated graduate school. God continues to use her to touch the lives of her staff and co-workers. She sees how God can use her in that place, not just to earn a living but as His ambassador. Gradually the zeal and joy of the Lord have returned in full blush for Pam.

There are still unanswered prayers. Her daughter, who rebelled against her mother and against God, has paid a big price for her rebellion. We continue to pray that she will finally come to the end of her rebellion and come back to God. We stand with Pam in the confidence that God is going to bring her daughter back to Himself and to a purposeful life.

Her son teeters on the fence between the life he knows is right and his own pursuits. But God is not through with him either, and we believe with Pam that his many talents and skills will yet be put to good use for the Lord.

THAT INCREDIBLE GRACE

As Pam puts it, 'I serve a wonderful Savior who in spite of my shortcomings and struggles, loves me and has good plans for me. I cannot say that everything has been roses. I can say that the Lord reigns.'

Our society, at given points in her life, would have placed Pam among some dismal statistics about children from one-parent homes, children who live in poverty, girls having babies, unwed mothers, drug abusers, broken homes. By all accounts Pam should have ended up on a dead-end street, hopeless and possibly destitute. She could easily have been a welfare mother, giving up on life and getting by as best she could. She could just as easily have become a prostitute in order to earn her living. She could have been a suicide statistic. But God saw a beautiful little girl who had been victimized, and even though the journey was difficult and painful, He brought her to a place of rest and joy. That is because He is a God of grace. Astonishing, marvelous grace.

4

RAHAB'S STORY

Rahab chose a lifestyle that gave her a bad name, and she had a hard time shaking it. Did you ever get a label pinned on you that you could not get rid of? Maybe it was the nickname you picked up as a kid. Perhaps instead of a name it was a reputation you could not seem to change. Your mother always said you were messy, and to this day she talks about how messy you are, even though you are not messy anymore. Maybe it was sleepy-headed, slow, the class nerd or clown that you were called. Labels can get old after a while.

I have to believe Rahab felt that way. She is mentioned in the Bible seven times, and five out of those seven times her name is linked with the label from her past: 'Rahab, the harlot,' or 'Rahab, the prostitute.' The label is there for all the world to know that she had a sordid and sinful past.

A DOUBLE-WHAMMY PAST

Rahab's story is found in Joshua chapter two. If you haven't read it lately, this is a good place to stop and do just that. It won't take long, and it is a very interesting story.

To the people of Israel, Rahab had two strikes against her: first, she was not a Jew, and second, she was an Amorite, a tribe known as enemies of the Jewish people. So Rahab was racially incorrect. Her profession also presented a problem; she earned her living through prostitution.

Rahab's house was built on the wall that surrounded Jericho and undoubtedly served as an inn, as well as a house of harlotry. She had a good marketing position for her trade, catching all the traveling merchants as they went in and out of Jericho. All the indications are that she lived alone, because she had to bring her family into her house at the time of the siege. It can be assumed that she owned that house. She was probably a successful business woman.

Though it was no less sinful in God's sight, prostitution in this godless land was an acceptable, if not prestigious way for a woman to make a living. In fact, temple prostitutes were given respect and thought of quite highly. (These were the prostitutes associated with the various temples of the many gods worshiped by the Amorites.) Rahab's profession, it would seem, was considered neither illegal nor particularly immoral.

However, it is important to point out that even though it was acceptable in the culture, it was still sinful and carried the consequences of sin. God's truth is unchanging, and even though people may try to whitewash sexual sin (premarital sex, adultery, homosexuality), it will never be possible to be rid of its consequences. In our culture we see proof of this.

Whether or not Rahab's occupation was acceptable in her society, it was not acceptable to God. Thankfully, according to Scripture, she was delivered from that profession.

A Shrewd Woman

One thing you have to hand Rahab the harlot – she was smart. Out of all the people who lived in Jericho, she was the only one who saw the changes coming, predicted the invasion of foreigners, and prepared for it. It reminds me of the parable Jesus taught in Luke 16:1-9, where the wasteful and unsatisfactory manager who is being fired by his boss is shrewd in taking steps to make certain that he has some income stability after he is fired. He goes to all his master's debtors and reduces their debts, so that they will be indebted to him. As a result, he will be able to call in his chips and be welcomed into their homes should he become homeless.

As Jesus tells this parable, the master commends this man for acting shrewdly. Jesus commented, 'For the people of this world are more shrewd in dealing with their own kind than are the people of the light' (Luke 16:8). These are strange words which I have puzzled over often, but it is clear that Jesus is commending shrewdness; not deceitfulness or dishonesty, but shrewdness. And Rahab was definitely shrewd in her dealings with the Jewish spies.

The spies went to Rahab's house for lodging. I imagine they wanted to appear to be the normal type of merchant travelers who would come in and out of the city, and staying at Rahab's place may have been considered an inconspicuous act that would not arouse suspicion. But if that was their plan, it did not work, because the king of Jericho learned they were there and ordered Rahab to bring out those spies.

But here is where her shrewdness took over. She pretended the men had come and gone, and told the king's messengers she did not know which way they went. She suggested they go quickly to find them before the men got too far away, and with that bit of playacting, she sent them on a wild-goose chase while she hid the spies on her rooftop.

RAHAB'S DEAL

After she got rid of the king's police who were looking for the spies, Rahab negotiated with these two Jewish men who were hiding on her roof under stalks of flax. She began:

> I know that the LORD has given this land to you and that a great fear of you has fallen on us, so that all who live in this country are melting in fear because of you (Josh. 2:9).

She went on to explain that she had heard of the mighty acts the Jewish God had performed and the battles the Israelites had won, and that her people were scared to death of a battle with the Jewish people.

However, I doubt that many others in Jericho agreed with Rahab that this land had been given to the Jews. After all, the Amorites had lived there for years and years. Why would the land belong to anyone else?

RAHAB'S FAITH

Rahab believed that the God of Israel was the true God and, believing that, she did not find it difficult to believe that the people of Israel would be able to defeat the Amorites and take over her land.

Faith and courage always come down to a question of what you really believe about God. Anyone who believes that God is the only God, all-powerful, all-knowing, all-wise and sovereign, as well as loving, gracious, merciful and long-suffering, should have no difficulty trusting God.

The Bible says God created the world in six days. It's not hard to believe if you believe He is God. He can create it in any way and in any time frame He chooses. Jesus walked on water; I have got no problem with that because I believe Jesus is who He said He was – God.

FAITH'S NECESSARY FOUNDATION

My problem is that my faith wavers. One day I believe I can tell a mountain to move and it will, and the next day I can hardly move myself. So, when my faith is weak, it needs to be reinforced with a fresh dose of who God really is. I often do that by talking out loud to myself – that is, when I can do so discreetly!

I will say, 'Mary, it comes down to this: Do you really believe God is God? If so, what is so difficult about believing that He can send a few dollars in to support the ministry He has entrusted to you?' (This is one of the greatest weak spots in my faith.) Or I will talk to myself this way, 'Mary, did God raise Jesus from the dead? Is that same power working in you, as the Bible says it is? Then how can you shake here in your boots from fear of failure, or your own inadequacy, or fear of the future?'

Our faith hinges on the depth of our belief in who God really is, and faith comes by the Word of God. Therefore, when I systematically and regularly put the Word of God into my mind through sermons, Bible study, good literature and Christian radio (just a little plug!), I have a reservoir of truth to strengthen my weak faith. Without that reservoir, I am susceptible to all kinds of ups and downs in my walk with God.

RAHAB'S RISKY PLAN

Rahab's faith was remarkable, because she had very little information on which to base it. She had heard about this God, she believed what she had heard, and she acted on the little knowledge and faith she had. Jesus said it does not take big faith to move mountains, just a willingness to exercise that little faith. Rahab was ready to take a chance on this God she had heard about; she was ready to make a total commitment even with that little bit of faith.

Think of the risk she took. If she turned out to be wrong about the God of Israel, she was putting herself and her family in grave danger by aligning herself with those spies and their God. She certainly ran a risk when she hid the spies; had they been discovered, she would have been guilty of treason, no doubt punishable by death. Her faith was strong and courageous because she truly believed that the God of Israel was indeed the true God.

I believe that somehow, throughout her life, Rahab had a deep longing to know the truth about God. I believe she somehow knew that the pagan gods of her people were not for real, and she desperately wanted to know the truth. When she heard the truth about this strange God who dried up the water of the Red Sea and destroyed Sihon and Og, two Amorite kings, her spirit testified to her.

Moses told the people years earlier:

> But if from there you seek the LORD your God, you will find Him if you look for Him with all your heart and with all your soul (Deut. 4:29).

Jeremiah repeated it years later:

> 'You will seek Me and find Me when you seek Me with all your heart. I will be found by you,' declares the LORD (Jer. 29:13-14).

Jesus repeated the same truth in His Sermon on the Mount:

> Ask and it will be given to you; seek and you will find; knock and the door will be opened to you (Matt. 7:7).

And the Apostle Paul stood up in the meeting of the Areopagus and said:

> God did this so that men would seek Him and perhaps reach out for Him and find Him, though He is not far from each one of us (Acts 17:27).

God loves to see people who really seek for Him. Nothing pleases Him more. A seeking heart will find God. I have seen that illustrated so often in the lives of people I know. Many of the contemporary stories in this book are further illustrations of how a seeking heart will somehow, some way, find the truth about God.

Many years ago, in my small Monday night Bible study, we prayed for the husband of one of the young women. Drew had not yet accepted Christ, and Renee was eager for him to see the light. Each week she updated us on his progress, as he came to church with her and asked questions. One night she told us he had decided to read the Bible all the way through to see if it were true. I remember saying to her, 'Renee, don't worry; Drew is seeking to know the truth about God. He will find God because God has promised that seeking hearts will find Him.'

The weeks went on, and Drew kept reading. After completing that lengthy assignment, he still was not certain of whether he could truly believe the Bible. I encouraged Renee to suggest that Drew meet with our pastor, for I felt it was time he discussed his questions with someone qualified to answer them.

Drew was willing to do that. He met with our pastor, asked some of his difficult questions, and was told that he could place his faith in God even though all his questions were not answered. Drew became a new creation in Christ.

You can count on it; when you see someone who is genuinely searching for the truth about God and willing to take action when he or she hears the truth, God will find His way into that person's life with His transforming truth. Rahab must have surely had that lifelong search to know the truth. So, even with her limited knowledge, she believed.

A SCARLET CORD

In return for protecting them, Rahab negotiated with the two spies that when the Israelites invaded her city, they would spare her and her family. They agreed that her home would be spared, provided she tied a scarlet cord through the window of her home. They gave her the scarlet cord to tie, and promised that if she kept her bargain and did not reveal their secret, she and everyone in her house would be spared when they invaded.

A scarlet cord – what a strange signal! How is it they happened to have a scarlet cord to give to Rahab? Why did they choose that? We are not given the direct answer to that question, but that scarlet ribbon is a wonderful picture of the blood of Jesus Christ, which must be applied to our lives if we are to be spared the condemnation we deserve. You see, Rahab deserved to be destroyed along with all her people. They were the enemy that God had told the children of Israel to completely destroy. They were occupying the land promised by God to His people. God had made it clear that this enemy must be destroyed, and Rahab was one of the enemy.

But a simple scarlet cord tied in the window would save her and her family from the judgment of God. No other cord would do; no other location would work. Rahab had explicit instructions that had to be followed to the letter if she wanted to be saved. It was easy enough to do – requiring no hard work on her part, no money, no lengthy period of time. But she had to follow the instructions exactly.

It reminds me of the instructions given to the people of God while in Egypt. They were told to put blood on the door posts, so that when the death angel saw the blood, he would pass over them and save them from death. Simple enough to do, but if that blood were not applied to the door posts at the appointed time, the death angel would visit their home. No exceptions. No substitutes. No alterations.

Both of these situations are such a beautiful picture of what we must do to be saved from the death we deserve. It is simple. It does not take long. It is available to anyone who so chooses. But the instructions are explicit and cannot be altered. It is not 'all roads lead to God.' There is only one road that leads to God, and it is the scarlet cord road. You must place your personal belief in Jesus Christ and the blood that He shed on Calvary for your sin. You must put that scarlet cord of faith in the window of your heart, for all the world to see that you are depending on the sacrifice of Jesus to save you from the penalty of death, which you deserve because you are a sinner.

Often people want to use substitutes. 'Let me put the cord of good works in my window. Surely that will be effective.' Or, 'I'll put the cord of church attendance or baptism in my window.' I honestly believe that some people would put the cord of pushing a peanut with their nose across the country if that were required, but they choke on the scarlet cord of the blood of Jesus Christ. Why? Because it takes simple faith, it takes a humble spirit, it takes a contrite heart, and for the proud heart of the natural person, that can be difficult to accept.

Rahab had to exercise incredible faith in that simple plan, and she did it without question and without hesitation. As soon as they reached their agreement, she tied that cord in the window. This shrewd woman recognized the way of escape when she heard it, and she placed her whole trust in that simple scarlet cord.

AN UNLIKELY ENDING

It worked out exactly the way they planned it. When the people of Israel crossed the Jordan and invaded Jericho, Joshua sent the same two spies to locate Rahab's house and rescue all who were in it. They brought out the entire family and put them in a place outside the camp of Israel before they burned the whole city.

> But Joshua spared Rahab the prostitute, with her family and all who belonged to her, because she hid the men Joshua had sent as spies to Jericho – and she lives among the Israelites to this day (Josh. 6:25).

Yes, she lived among the Israelites for the rest of her days, but the story gets better. Not only was she spared the death she deserved, but a romance developed between her and Salmon. We do not know much about Salmon; maybe he was one of the spies that rescued Rahab and saw in her that seeking heart and gentle spirit. At any rate, Rahab's life was dramatically changed; she escaped the death she deserved and was chosen to be the wife of Salmon. All she expected was to live in safety, perhaps as an outcast or a foreigner among the Israelites; she would have been grateful for any place in society. But in a most unlikely ending, Rahab was taken in as one of the chosen, married Salmon and gave birth to Boaz, the father of Obed, the father of Jesse, the father of King David.

Rahab was forever changed by God's astonishing grace. We do not need to call her 'Rahab the prostitute'; the label no longer applies. She became a new creation and life took on meaning and righteousness.

'IMMEASURABLY MORE' GRACE

Here is one of the best passages in the whole Bible:

> Now to Him who is able to do immeasurably more than all we ask or imagine, according to His power that is at work within us,

to Him be glory in the church and in Christ Jesus throughout all generations, for ever and ever! Amen (Eph. 3:20–21).

I am sure Rahab would agree about that passage from Ephesians, because God did immeasurably more for her than she could ever have dreamed, imagined or asked. She is listed in the eleventh chapter of Hebrews, the Bible's 'Hall of Faith', right along with Abraham, Moses, Noah and all the great Bible names of faith: 'By faith the prostitute Rahab, because she welcomed the spies, was not killed with those who were disobedient' (Heb. 11:31). Sarah is the only other woman listed in this famous chapter. What an ending for a woman who had a sordid past as a harlot!

Do you see how deep and wide God's grace is? God did not just want to save Rahab and her family from destruction; He wanted to make something beautiful out of her life and give her a place in history such as few other women have ever known.

We are often willing to settle for so much less than God is willing to do for us. Knowing our unworthiness, knowing our past, knowing our weaknesses and failures, knowing our inadequacies, we assume that God would treat us the way we treat others or ourselves. Oh, He might pull us up out of that miry pit, clean the mud off and make us acceptable, perhaps even respectable. But something glorious? It never enters our minds.

If you can just get a better glimpse of God's grace, you will realize that because of *who* He is, you have the potential of doing and being more than you have yet asked or imagined. This is not New Age 'you can do anything you want to do' philosophy; nor is it pride or self-confidence. It is rather a true understanding of the transforming power of the grace of God in a life that has been set free from the past.

It simply does not matter what your past has been, God has a place in His 'Hall of Faith' for you. He wants to show the world the glory of His grace by doing in and through you more than you have ever dreamed. Please do not settle for anything less.

Let me tell you about another woman, who has put her past behind her because of God's astonishing grace.

5

KAREN'S STORY

Unlike Rahab, Karen's early years gave her a good start and excellent potential for a fruitful life of service to the Lord. She came to saving faith as a 13-year-old through a camp ministry, and until she was twenty, her life was centered on pleasing God and following His plan for her life. She was discipled by a young Messianic Jewish man and his wife, and attended weekly Bible studies, where she was tutored in sound doctrine and Christian living. She memorized Scripture, had a consistent prayer life, sang in a Christian music group, actively engaged in evangelistic events, and joined a mission that focused its outreach to the Jewish people. After high school, she attended Moody Bible Institute in Chicago, fully intending to invest her life in some type of ministry.

Everyone – including Karen – expected her life to follow the obvious path as she had begun, yet sadly, as she entered her twenties, she became obsessed by her childhood desire to have a relationship with a man and get married. From the time when she saw *Sleeping Beauty* at age five, Karen was enraptured with the idea of being rescued by Prince Charming. There was never a time in her impressionable young life, even in Kindergarten, when she did not have a 'crush' on somebody, yearning for someone to take note of her and make her dream come true.

However, she had to wear corrective shoes as she grew up, which did not enhance her appearance, and she was thirty pounds overweight, so, in her words, 'I was never what the boys were looking for.' At age twenty she had never been to a prom and had been on only one date – and a disastrous one at that. The loneliness she felt became overwhelming. Karen firmly believed that God would send her this man of her dreams, but He did not. Her lack of being loved was so unbearable – like being denied oxygen – that she left Moody Bible Institute after completing her second year and moved back home. That is when her life began to fall apart, as she determined to find love anyhow and at any cost.

THE ROAD DOWNHILL

Not finding someone to love her in her Christian community, Karen began hanging around in bars with her older sister and her friends. If Christian men would not give her the time of day, she found other men who did. She lost thirty pounds, let her hair grow long, and uncovered her good looks. She found that she was popular with these new friends, and that was a better high than the marijuana and other 'fun drugs' that she was taking at that time. Her phone was constantly ringing with some guy wanting to spend more time with her. At last Karen had the attention she had craved for so long, and her starving for affection was over.

Also gone were her innocence and her desire to serve God. She became completely engulfed in sex, drugs and thrill-seeking. Though she still had not found that Prince Charming – that one man to love her completely – she had found a substitute that felt good for a while, mistaking the one night stands and the excitement of being desirable for true love. Life was exciting, with one emotional high after another. The thrills were enough for a time.

Hebrews 11:25 talks about the fleeting pleasures of sin, and gradually Karen began to recognize this truth. As the years went by, her alcohol and drug consumption went from 'just partying' to being completely out of control. Instead of dealing with the pain inside her, she was pushing it further down inside. She began attending culinary school, but sold drugs to supplement her income and worked as a cocktail waitress at a well-known Irish pub. How quickly and how steeply she had traveled this downhill path!

THE WORST HOURS OF HER LIFE

One Friday night, after waitressing in the cocktail lounge, Karen went to a four o'clock bar with a guy and experienced her first alcoholic blackout. After drinking and playing pinball, the next thing she remembers is driving in her car and making a right hand turn the wrong way down a one-way street, right in front of a police car.

They pulled her over and could smell the joint she had just smoked. If they had opened her door, she would have spilled out onto the street. In her words, she was 'sloshed.'

For reasons unknown to her, they did not arrest her, but merely gave her a ticket and told her to sleep it off. She must have fallen asleep in her car, and as daylight broke, she tried to find her way home and got lost. She was hungry, so she stopped at a convenience store for a snack. She left her purse in the car and took only her keys and some change into the store.

She was so blind drunk that she could not find her way back to her car and could not even read the street signs that were two feet in front of her. She had no idea of how long she tried to find her way back to her car, but the next thing she knew, she looked down and saw that her wraparound skirt had come untied and was missing. She was staggering around the side streets of Chicago in a black slip and her little waitress apron.

The shame and degradation of that moment still haunts her. With her last twenty cents, she found a pay phone and called her boyfriend to come and get her. But in her blind confusion, she told him the wrong street corner because she was still too blind to read the signs correctly. Finally she collapsed in a heap right there on the street corner, crying and looking like a rape victim. She was frightened and in total despair, not knowing what to do.

At that most embarrassing moment, two young men approached her and said, 'Miss, we are students at the Moody Bible Institute and we attend Moody Church, and you look like you could use some help.' What an incredible divine intervention! Even in her drunken state, she recognized the sovereignty of God, and even though she had turned her back on Him, she felt His love and care for her. To their amazement, she told the young men that she was a born-again Christian and had even attended MBI and Moody Church. But it was not easy to explain the condition she was in at that moment.

They drove her home and helped her in this terrible hour of need. Karen attended church with them for the next two Sundays, but still she was not ready to give God control of her life. That night had cost her dearly; she lost all the money she had made that night waitressing, as well as the entire contents of her purse including all her identification and her prescription glasses. In addition, in her drunken stupor she thought her car had been stolen because she could not remember where she parked it. It turned up in the police compound many months later, after she had bought another car. But even more costly than that was the guilt, which she now found unbearable. 'I often wonder if it would have been less painful to have been arrested by the police and to have spent the night in jail for drunk driving,' Karen now says.

DEEPENING ADDICTIONS

In her refusal to relinquish control of her life to God, Karen's addictions grew stronger. She couldn't get through a day without cigarettes, drugs and alcohol. Cocaine became her most popular drug, and since her boyfriend was a dealer, it was readily available to her at all times. Realizing that she got into less trouble by doing her drugs at home rather than the party scene, she began to live like a recluse – a typical stage in most addictions.

In addition to her other addictions, her found herself addicted to food, using it as a way to further numb herself and shut down all her feelings. This led to a lot of weight gain, and Karen's life was unraveling even further. She became dysfunctional and truly wanted to die.

She began a nine-year live-in relationship with a violent man who was also an alcoholic. This live-in relationship was the furthest thing from the love she so longed for. The man had a personality that could change in a matter of seconds if his authority was challenged. To avoid hours of endless fighting, Karen learned to tip-toe around him in order to avoid upsetting him in any way. He assaulted her physically and verbally, but for her the verbal was the most painful.

Karen clearly remembers his words of abuse, like, 'You are so unattractive, you do not even have to worry about being raped,' and when he put his gun to her temple and threatened to pull the trigger, she told him to go ahead; he would be doing her a favor. She meant it. Life was no longer worth living. She did not have the courage to end her own life, but she wished her life would end.

FINALLY ASKING FOR HELP

Unlike many addicts, Karen was not living in denial. She knew that her life was a total disaster; she knew she was an alcoholic and needed help. Finally she was getting to the point where she was ready to do something about it. By the grace of God, this live-in boyfriend was ready to get some help as well.

Soon she took her last drink, and they both began attending AA meetings. She took a long look at what she had done with her life and felt the shame and disgrace. The one thing that led her down this sin-infested path – that once-in-a-lifetime relationship she had so yearned for – had never been realized, and she finally saw that she had rejected God's control in her life for nothing.

Sitting in an AA meeting, she began contemplating the third step advocated by that organization, which involves turning your life and your will over to your 'higher power,' as they call it. For Karen this 'higher power' was personal – it was the one true God and his Son, Jesus Christ. Regardless of the life she had led, she knew that she was still a child of God and never doubted her eternal security.

Turning her life over to the Lord was still a hurdle for Karen. She told God she was not yet willing, but she was willing to be made willing to give control of her life back to Him. She began to miss the wonderful things she enjoyed in her youth as a young Christian. She missed singing the old hymns, sitting in church and listening to a good sermon; the joy of sharing the gospel with others. Her journey back to God had begun.

RETURNING TO THE LORD

Karen stopped doing speed and cocaine, because it made her desire a drink to balance out the high, and she knew she did not want to start drinking again. So the drugs had to go. Her job schedule changed so that she no longer had to work on Sundays, and she went straight back to Moody Church, sitting in the back to be as inconspicuous as possible. She even began to read God's Word again, much to the dismay of her boyfriend.

As the weeks passed, Karen rarely missed a Sunday church service and by now she was sitting in the front row and hanging on every word of the sermon. It was, in her words, 'pure ecstasy' to hear God's word expounded again. She could not get enough.

Now her prayer was to get away from this man she was still stuck with. Since he was sober, things were a bit better, but he still loved to poke fun at her when she was reading God's Word. But this was what gave her the strength to ignore him when he became obnoxious.

Finally came the wonderful day when she moved to another apartment, and it was like breaking out of chains or getting out of prison. Now that he was history, she did not have to be around the marijuana anymore and it was easier to say goodbye to that sin. She began memorizing Scripture again, and her desire to serve the Lord returned.

FINDING COMPLETE VICTORY

Even though she had made major changes in her life, Karen still had quite a bit of work to do on herself. She was now 100 pounds overweight and in bad health, and she was still secluding herself. At this point she recognized her need to go to another twelve-step program for her food addiction, as she had with AA. So, began attending Overeaters Anonymous. In a little over a year, she lost the 100 pounds, and the emotional and spiritual healing she so desperately needed was happening.

Her favorite addiction, smoking cigarettes, was the last one to go – and amazingly she was able to quit that habit without any nicotine withdrawal or weight gain. Karen was astonished to realize that her addictions were behind her. She went from bad health to excellent health by the power of God's Spirit. Her life was given back to her, and she once again began walking with God in complete obedience and joy.

Karen says, 'God has given me back my life. What a merciful God we serve, who would bless me and restore my life to me in spite of my unfaithfulness to Him.'

THE EPILOGUE

I have been privileged to watch Karen as she has transitioned back from a life that was lost and desperate to a life full of meaning and joy. She is a blessing to many people, and has a compassionate heart for those caught in addictions as she was. God uses her to touch many lives, and you can see the joy in her eyes as she continues to walk with the Lord.

As she became active in Moody Church, God brought her the man of her dreams – reminiscent of Rahab's story as she married Salmon. She met Tom at church, and their friendship led to a marriage after almost two years. They both treasure their relationship with the Lord and with each other. He is the adoring husband she always wanted. He gets up much earlier than he would otherwise have to in order to read Scripture with her before she leaves for work. Then he walks her down to the car to say goodbye as she goes to her job at, of all places, Moody Bible Institute!

God's grace is astonishing and abundant, and Karen is living proof!

6

RUTH'S STORY

Ruth always tried to do the right thing. She was a good girl, who had a very difficult life. Goethe, the German poet, dramatist and novelist, has called the Book of Ruth 'the loveliest little idyll that tradition has transmitted to us' (Edith Dean, *All the Women of the Bible*, p. 85). If Ruth could hear her story described this way, I think she would be appalled. First, it is a true story with real people, not an idyllic composition of pastoral scenes and a charming story. Second, it was not passed on by tradition; it was written by an unknown author under the inspiration of God's Holy Spirit. It has been transmitted to us not to give us a lovely piece of prose, but 'to teach us, so that through endurance and the encouragement of the Scriptures we might have hope' (Rom. 15:4).

I certainly do agree with Goethe that it is a lovely story. Ruth is a woman we can all admire and emulate. She stands tall among all the women in the Bible for her integrity, her loyalty, her gentle spirit, her submission to God's will, her hard work, and her uncomplaining attitude.

Ruth's story is a love story. Who doesn't enjoy a love story – especially when it ends as well as Ruth's did? But in order to appreciate the ending, we need to take another look at how Ruth's story began and what she went through. You will find her story (where else?) in the book of Ruth in the Old Testament. It is a short book and very easy to read. You may want to read it once again – or for the first time – as you begin this chapter.

NAOMI'S PLIGHT

Elimelech, his wife Naomi, and their two sons, Mahlon and Kilion, were of the Jewish tribe of Judah. They lived in Bethlehem near Jerusalem as part of God's people. However, a famine came to the land and Elimelech decided to move to Moab, about 120 miles away. In Ruth 1:3 we read that Elimelech died there. Naomi, now an older widow, had to somehow provide for herself and her two sons. A younger widow could go back to her father's home for shelter, but an older widow whose parents were dead had to depend on her children for support. Naomi's sons were still young, and she was nowhere near her family, even if they were still alive.

Eventually, Naomi's sons married Moabite women. The boys took care of their mother, and she got along well with her two daughters-in-law, Ruth and Orpah. She had her family together and they were managing to put food on the table. I'm sure she missed Bethlehem and her people, and it must have been very difficult to live in this foreign land without her husband, but she survived and made the best of the situation for ten years.

Until her worst nightmare came true. Both of her boys died. Not one, but both. How much grief can one woman take? What happened to fairness? Where was God in all this? Did Naomi deserve this kind of devastation? No doubt those thoughts went through her mind.

You know, when we're going through deep waters, our minds will question God too. I really don't think God objects; He is big enough to stand up under our scrutiny and our questions and even our doubts. What must disappoint Him is to see one of His children continue in that state of disbelief and distrust.

NAOMI PREPARES TO GO HOME

After the loss of her husband and sons, Naomi's heart turned to her home. She heard that there was now food in Bethlehem and she prepared to go back. Both daughters-in-law prepared to go with her. You see, according to tradition, as we saw with Tamar, these two Moabite women were to marry another son in Elimelech's family so that they could bear children to carry on the names of Naomi's two dead sons. It seems that neither of them had any children. This means that the line of Elimelech would cease unless one of these girls could produce a son for her dead husband. It was quite a dilemma for Naomi, who was now old and not likely to marry again or have any more children.

The three of them set out for Judah, which had to be a long and arduous journey by foot or donkey, but as they got started, it seemed that Naomi had a change of heart. Undoubtedly, she would have loved for these girls to return with her. They were all she had left of a family; they were her only ties to her sons. Yet she realized how wrong it was to ask them to go back to a foreign land, leaving their families, where they would have little chance of finding a husband.

> Return home, my daughters. Why would you come with me? Am I going to have any more sons, who could become your husbands? Return home, my daughters; I am too old to have another husband. Even if I thought there was still hope for me – even if I had a husband tonight and then gave birth to sons – would you wait until they grew up? Would you remain unmarried for them? No, my daughters (Ruth 1:11-13).

'I've got nothing to offer you,' Naomi said to Orpah and Ruth. 'Do the practical thing; look out for yourself. Return to your families.' It sure makes sense to me, how about you? I am afraid I would have seen it the way Orpah did. She kissed her mother-in-law good-bye and went back. But not Ruth.

RUTH'S RESPONSE

It is difficult for us in today's culture to fully appreciate the decision that Ruth made. She refused to go back home and insisted on staying with Naomi, returning to Bethlehem to live with her there. Her beautiful words to Naomi have been quoted (out of context, by the way, but no harm done) in many wedding ceremonies:

> Don't urge me to leave you or to turn back from you. Where you go I will go, and where you stay I will stay. Your people will be my people and your God my God. Where you die I will die, and there I will be buried. May the LORD deal with me, be it ever so severely, if anything but death separates you and me (Ruth 1:16-17).

Just to hear the words she spoke gives you an insight into this Moabite woman. She may have been from a pagan nation, but she had a heart of love and purity. Her devotion to Naomi was remarkable, which says a lot about Naomi too. Such a bond developed between them that Ruth wanted to accept not only Naomi's land as her dwelling-place, but her God as well.

This was no trite, spur-of-the-moment decision; this was a life-changing choice for Ruth. The prospects for her were dismal. To go with Naomi back to Bethlehem not only meant leaving behind everything and everyone dear to her, but it also meant living in a foreign culture among strange people for the rest of her life.

In addition to simply changing cultures, Ruth was going to live with Naomi, a widow who had no home, no means of support, and no family to take care of her. There were no social security safety nets in those days, no welfare, no Salvation Army soup lines. Ruth and Naomi were two very poor, very alone women in a world built for men, and their prospects of finding anyone to support or help them were bleak at best.

No doubt Ruth understood the enormity of her decision, but with unwavering determination, she entreated Naomi not to even talk about sending her back to Moab. This was a very strong lady: strong in her self-sacrifice, strong in her loyalty, and strong in her persuasion. Naomi no longer argued with her, and they started the long journey back to Bethlehem.

THE REALITY OF HOME

Once they reached Bethlehem, their presence caused a stir. 'Can this be Naomi?' her friends in town exclaimed. I imagine she had aged a great deal. The gray hair, the lines in her face, the dirt and grime of the journey clinging to her clothes must have shocked those who knew her in better times.

Immediately Naomi and Ruth had to worry about where their next meal was coming from. No meals were delivered by the church hospitality committee; they were on their own.

I would have sat down and had a good cry about this time. The pity party would have been in full swing, had it been me instead of Ruth. After all they had been through, these two women still had to fend for themselves. But Ruth refused to feel sorry for herself; she refused to quit. Naomi tasted the fruit of bitterness; she insisted on being called Mara, not Naomi, because Mara means bitter, and her life had become bitter. She blamed it on the Lord in her moment of despair. Ruth simply got busy doing something.

I have noticed that one of the best remedies for self-pity and depression is to get busy doing something. I'm not suggesting that you bury your head in activity and refuse to face reality, but sometimes the best way to pull yourself out of the dumps is just to do something worthwhile. It might be scrubbing the floor, cleaning the house, writing a book, typing a report, or anything else that needs to be done. Just getting going with some activity is often my first step in changing my attitude and stopping the pity party. The first step is hard, but once you get going, you discover that you can usually regain your equilibrium pretty quickly.

Since it was barley harvest time, Ruth said to Naomi, 'Let me go to the fields and pick up the leftover grain behind anyone in whose eyes I find favor' (Ruth 2:2). Here again we need some understanding of the ancient customs. Widows or even resident aliens had the right by law to gather grain anywhere they pleased (Lev.19:9; 23:22; Deut. 24:19). According to Old Testament law, landowners were instructed not to reap their fields completely to the corners, but to leave some gleanings in the fields for the widows and aliens who were in need. It was God's welfare program, making provision for the poor. (Note that the poor had to gather the grain, so they put their own sweat equity into this program.)

This provision to allow poor people to glean the fields was not to be seen as their right. Rather, it was a provision of God's grace, to be received by those in need with thankfulness and appreciation. Never in Scripture is there any indication that God evaluates people by how much they have; but He does expect those who have to share with those who have not.

RUTH'S HARD WORK

Try to put yourself in Ruth's position. She is so poor that she must glean in the fields. This immediately identifies her to everyone in town as a destitute woman. Besides, she is an outsider. I doubt if many people were even willing to speak to her, so I imagine that she gleaned those fields quite alone. She was a Moabitess; she wasn't part of the in-crowd.

But Ruth stayed focused on the task at hand – finding enough food for herself and her mother-in-law. Gleaning the fields was hard, back-breaking work. It was done in the very hot sun, by bending over and meticulously picking up the leftovers. It must have been similar to picking cotton in the hot Southern sun. My back hurts just thinking about it. It was also dangerous work for a woman by herself. We know from Boaz's later words (Ruth 2:9) and Naomi's to Ruth (Ruth 2:22) that a woman gleaning alone in the fields was vulnerable to harm, probably rape.

How humiliating for Ruth! How exhausting. Was this what her life was to be from now on? I think she was fully aware that she could be in this type of predicament forever, because there was no obvious source of help. But without complaining, without blaming God, without taking it out on Naomi, she simply did what her hands found to do – she gleaned the fields for barley.

A REAL 'KNIGHT IN SHINING ARMOR'

Now the fairy tale begins. Along comes Boaz. I like this guy. He was a kind and considerate employer. In Ruth 2:4 he greets and blesses those working for him, and they return his blessing. Certainly he seemed to have good relationships with those he hired, and they respected him. He did not begrudge giving gleaners, such as Ruth, his grain; quite the opposite, he was glad to help.

Boaz was a man of God. He was undoubtedly wealthy, and he could have married any eligible young woman in town. Yet here he was, as far as we can tell, single and unattached. (I know all single women are saying to themselves right now, 'There aren't any of those around these days!')

In her wildest dreams Ruth could not have imagined marrying a man like Boaz. I doubt she even had hopes of any marriage. She was simply where she was supposed to be, doing what she was supposed to be doing, and Boaz noticed her.

Another lesser man might have immediately dismissed her because of her status. She was obviously very poor, and she couldn't have looked too great, working in the hot sun. What attracted Boaz to Ruth? He found out from his foreman that Ruth was the Moabitess woman who had returned with Naomi, and that she had been working steadily all day with only a short break. So, before he spoke to her, he knew that she was a foreigner, that she was poor, that she was diligent and hard-working.

It would seem that Boaz looked beyond the surface and saw the real Ruth. Lots of men have trouble looking beyond the exterior, and they often get involved with the wrong woman for the wrong reasons. External beauty is often too high on their list of qualifications. We do not know how Ruth looked, but I believe Boaz saw beyond the outward appearance and recognized in Ruth a woman of inner beauty and strength like none other he had met.

So, in great compassion, he spoke to Ruth and told her to please glean in his fields and his only. He assured her of protection from any harm in his fields, provided for her to have water any time she wanted, and made certain that his workers would leave stalks from the bundles for her to pick up.

Ruth immediately acknowledged his gracious help: 'Why have I found such favor in your eyes that you notice me – a foreigner?' (Ruth 2:10). She was well aware of her place in this society and recognized how unusual it was for anyone to be concerned for a foreigner, especially this man of such wealth and renown. I love Boaz's reply:

> I've been told all about what you have done for your mother-in-law since the death of your husband – how you left your father and mother and your homeland and came to live with a people you did not know before. May the LORD repay you for what you have done. May you be richly rewarded by the LORD, the God of Israel, under whose wings you have come to take refuge (Ruth 2:11-12).

If you are thinking Boaz is unusual, I have to agree. But he is a clear representation of our kinsman-redeemer, Jesus Christ. In his dealings with Ruth, we can see such a beautiful picture of how Jesus deals with us. We don't deserve His attention, and we are totally unworthy of His help and His provision, yet with tenderness beyond description He notices us, and He stoops to our need.

NAOMI'S PLAN

Naomi encouraged Ruth to continue gleaning in Boaz's fields where she would find protection. So Ruth stayed close to Boaz's servant girls and gleaned until the barley and wheat harvests were finished. It was hard work, but Boaz made it much easier for Ruth, and no doubt she and Naomi were counting their blessings. They had food, and someone seemed to care about their plight.

One day, when the harvest was over, Naomi encouraged Ruth to get dressed up, put on her best perfume, and go down to the threshing floor where Boaz was. Now, Naomi's plan sounds very strange to our ears. She told Ruth to lie low until Boaz had eaten and was relaxing for the evening. Then she was to go to him, uncover his feet, and lie down at his feet.

Certainly she was counting on Ruth being attractive to Boaz; it would not have made sense for Ruth to go there looking disheveled or dirty. In other words, she was doing everything she could to help things along, but she was operating within the boundaries of accepted behavior. There was nothing illegal, immoral, or even suggestive about this plan.

I admire Ruth, the Moabitess, for her willingness to present herself, as it were, to this wealthy Jewish man. She was gutsy enough to do it. As Boaz lay down to rest, she quietly made her way to his feet, uncovered them, and lay there at his feet. In the night he woke up to discover this woman at his feet, and she identified herself and asked him to spread his garment over her. This refers to the Jewish tradition of a husband covering his bride with the end of his prayer shawl as a symbolic gesture that she is under his protection (Ezek. 16:8). What she was doing was asking him, as a kinsman of her late husband, to marry her.

He fully understood the meaning of her request, and it did not distress him at all. In fact, he had nothing but kind words for her, and assured her that he was willing to take her as his bride. However, he explained that there was another male relative closer in relationship than he was, and he must first ask this other kinsman if he intended to marry Ruth. If not, Boaz assured her that he would marry her.

THE HAPPY ENDING

In the most honorable way imaginable, Boaz went to the city gate and met with the other kinsman who had first rights to Elimelech's property, including Ruth. After a discussion, the other kinsman insisted that he was not able to buy Elimelech's property and gave his right to Boaz. In front of witnesses, Boaz declared his intention to marry Ruth and care for her.

Not long thereafter a son was born to Ruth and Boaz, and Naomi cuddled him in her arms. This was the grandchild denied to her for so long; this was the one who would carry on her family name. She was overjoyed, and the women of the town were singing a new song to her:

Praise be to the LORD, who this day has not left you without a kinsman-redeemer. May he become famous throughout Israel! He will renew your life and sustain you in your old age. For your daughter-in-law, who loves you and who is better to you than seven sons, has given him birth (Ruth 4:14–15).

Indeed this new baby did bring great joy and comfort to Naomi and Ruth and Boaz. They named him Obed, and he was the father of Jesse, the father of David.

How could this Moabitess woman come out of nowhere – a nobody – and end up being the great-grandmother of David? Grace. God's incredible, amazing, astonishing grace. What a story!

GRACE WORTH WAITING FOR

Ruth had to wait quite a long time before she saw the results of God's grace in her life. By faith she had to go with Naomi and endure much pain and hardship before the evidence of grace came to her through Boaz. Suppose she had turned back on the road to Bethlehem – she could have done so at any point, and Naomi would not have stopped her. Suppose she had refused the degrading job of gleaning in the fields and decided to go back home – that was another possibility. Suppose she had left the field early that day before Boaz saw her – then the story would have had a different ending.

God's grace to you may yet be on its way. Isaiah 30:18 tells us: 'Yet the LORD longs to be gracious to you; He rises to show you compassion. For the LORD is a God of justice. Blessed are all who wait for Him!' None of us like the waiting part, but God often waits so that He can give us His best. Remember Ruth when you are tired of waiting to see God's grace in your life. Boaz was worth waiting for. And whatever it is that God has in His plan for you, I can wholeheartedly assure you, it is worth waiting for! Do not settle for anything less than the fullness of His marvelous grace. He has promised to bless you, if you will wait for Him.

In the next chapter you will read about Fran – a contemporary woman who also struggled with family issues. Like Ruth she discovered grace through a man who was kind to her.

7

FRAN'S STORY

Statistically she fits into the 'senior citizen' category, but Fran has a face, figure, and attitude thirty years younger than her age. She is an example of improving with age.

Like Ruth, Fran always tried to do the right thing. She too was a good girl who had a very difficult life.

A POOR BEGINNING

Before the word was fashionable, Fran knew what it meant to have a dysfunctional family. Her mother married when she was eighteen, which was not so unusual seventy years ago, but she married a man thirty-one years her senior. That was unusual, and as is almost always the case in such marriages, it provided a breeding ground for disaster.

Seven children were born to this summer/winter marriage, and though the house was run-down and shabby, they managed to live together in a normal fashion in a big Kansas town. Fran was the third child in the family, with two older sisters, two younger sisters, and two younger brothers. Their dad worked very hard to provide for his large, late-in-life family, and did his best for all the kids. He was a strong man, both physically and emotionally, so things held together pretty well.

Until, that is, he had a stroke that completely debilitated him, and all the family responsibility fell to Fran's mother, who was still young and not equipped to raise seven children by herself. Fran was ten years old when her father had the stroke.

Since he was no longer able to walk and could not take care of himself, Fran's mother took the only course of action she saw possible: she put her husband, now in his late 60s, in the county hospital. Without any preparation, their father was simply gone from the home. No explanation. From this point on, life became a living nightmare for Fran and her brothers and sisters.

A TERRORIZED CHILDHOOD

Confused and bewildered by the turn of events in her life, Fran's mother looked for escape in a bottle. She had been entirely dependent on her husband for financial and emotional stability, and with his absence, she seemed totally unable to cope with the huge responsibility now facing her. Even though she had not been a drinker before, the local beer joint provided a place for her to find attention and flattery from men, and she felt a need to have that kind of male support. So she began to spend most of her time in this cheap neighborhood tavern, which was a little over a mile from their home.

Not able to afford child-care, at first Fran's mother brought the kids along with her and they played in a corner of the tavern until the wee hours of the morning, while she drank with various men. Fran clearly recalls the long, barefoot walks to that tavern each night, and the long walks home, often carrying a sleeping brother or sister in her arms.

The children ranged in age from two to sixteen at that time, and the younger ones were only vaguely aware of their mother's social habits at the tavern, drinking and flirting with a continuous succession of men. Fran was eleven years old, and therefore somewhat more aware of the inappropriate surroundings of the tavern and the improper behavior of her mother. However, like her brothers and sisters, she figured that if her mother took her there, it must be okay.

Fran noticed that occasionally one of those men would walk home with them in the early morning hours, and he would still be there when she went to sleep with her brothers and sisters. Childhood can sometimes provide the blessing of ignorance and innocence, so at first she did not think too much about the implications of these male visitors.

Later on, her mother would sometimes leave the children at home by themselves when she went on her drinking binges. One morning the children found her passed out on the railroad track, never making it home because she was so drunk.

Many nights Fran's mother would have nightmares brought on by the alcohol, and she would scream with horror over the snakes that were all over her in her dream. She would yell at Fran to get the snakes off her. These memories of her mother's drunken nightmares still haunt Fran whenever she sees a picture of a snake.

It was not long before two or three of these men her mother met at the tavern would accompany her home when drinking hours were over. The younger brothers and sisters typically slept through the night in oblivion, but Fran was old enough to be aware of and terrified by the screams of her two older sisters and the shouts and laughter of her mother and her visitors.

These visitors became regular, and each night Fran's older sisters were taken from the communal bedroom, where all the kids slept together, into other parts of the house, to be used by her mother's drunken friends, while their mother was occupied in her own bedroom. Without full knowledge of what was happening, Fran knew enough to know it was wrong and it was evil. Her sisters never told her anything about these escapades, but the terror in their eyes and the screams in the night said enough. (It is Fran's opinion that they never realized it was wrong since they were simply doing what their mom told them to do.)

TAKING DRASTIC ACTION

Instinctively, Fran knew something had to be done about this ever-increasing horror that went on in her home each night. The only authority figure she trusted was her teacher, and she decided to tell her about the situation. The teacher was understandably shocked to hear Fran's frightful story and took her to the school principal.

For most children, being sent to the principal's office was not a positive experience, and Fran expected a good bawling out. To her surprise, this male figure became her friend and ally and said he wanted to help her. He made arrangements for Fran to phone the sheriff the next time a similar incident occurred. He informed Fran's neighbors that she might need to use their phone in the middle of the night at some time, and they agreed to allow her to do that. Fran had become a playmate of their daughter and they had been kind to Fran, although they never allowed any of the other children to come into their home. So Fran was prepared to run to the neighbor's home and call the sheriff.

Then, just a few nights later, after another night of drinking, her mother demanded that Fran 'entertain' the teenaged son of one of her visitors. She was only twelve years old at the time, and she refused to do what her mother demanded. In a drunken furor, her mother slapped Fran hard, throwing her across the bed.

Fran knew it was time to act, so she slipped out of the house and ran barefoot across the large cornfield that lay between her house and the neighbor's to call the sheriff. Her young mind did not consider what the results of that phone call would mean to her and her family. She simply knew that what was going on in her home was wrong, and she had to help her sisters.

Just as she crept back into her bed, unnoticed by her mother and her visitors, she saw the flashing lights of the sheriff's car outside. Fran trembled in her bed as the sheriff knocked on the front door, then went around to the rear and broke down the back door to her home. Her mother was arrested on the spot, and the authorities confiscated all the evidence needed to prosecute her for contributing to the delinquency of minors.

THE FAMILY SPLIT

At her mother's trial, Fran was the only one of the children called to testify. Not until then did her family know that she was the one who had called the sheriff. Testifying in that intimidating courtroom against her own mother was something Fran will never forget, even though it was many years ago. She had to face her mother, sitting at the table in front of her, and recite the details of her behavior. It was shameful and embarrassing, as well as frightening. She remembers concentrating so hard to try to understand the questions, and she sensed that the prosecution was not always satisfied with her answers, as they probed for more details. All Fran could think of was getting it over with and getting out of there as fast as she could.

But even with the great fear that gripped her, she still knew that what had been going on in her home was wrong and had to be stopped. At the time, however, she did not understand that her testimony would ensure her mother's conviction and send her to prison, and she certainly never imagined that it would cause the breakup of her family.

But that is exactly what happened – the family would never be together again as a family unit. It was dysfunctional, true, but it was her family and, in Fran's mind, she was responsible for breaking up their home. Guilt and shame covered her like a blanket and haunted her for years and years.

With her mother in jail, Fran's oldest sister was sent to a reform school in order to prevent her from following in her mother's footsteps. Because of severe epilepsy, her next oldest sister was sent to a state hospital – the only place the state had for children to be treated at that time. The remaining five were kept temporarily in a detention home. Through no fault of their own, these precious children were sent in different directions, and they had to endure the consequences of their mother's sin.

Eventually the baby in the family was adopted, and Fran's two brothers and other sister were situated in different foster homes. Fran remained in the detention home.

To add to her guilt, Fran's father died a few months after her mother's arrest, and all the children were allowed to attend his funeral. When Fran saw her mother there, she felt so ashamed that she did not want to speak to her. At that moment she decided that she would have nothing more to do with her mother and would avoid seeing her or communicating with her as much as possible. A combination of anger and guilt drove a huge wedge into her heart, and though her mother was released from prison after one year, Fran did not see her again for over thirty years.

Her mother never again had custody of any of her children, and she went back into her former life of alcohol and illicit relationships. She lived with one man for quite a few years, though they never married. In fact, his invalid wife lived in the same house with them. It was not a pretty life for Fran's mother. Though she lived for some time in the same vicinity as her mother, Fran kept her vow never to have any contact with her. It was a past she wanted to forget.

LIFE ON HER OWN

Fran lived at the detention home for a while, and then the State authorities found her a job washing dishes in a local hospital. For this she was given a room at the hospital as well as her meals. All of her siblings were placed in homes right away, but not Fran. Her young mind concluded that her punishment for breaking up the family was that she would never have a family again and would always be alone.

This was where she lived until her freshman year in high school. At that time she was placed with a foster family, about 30 miles out of town, and lived with them for one year. They had a daughter Fran's age, and the two were good friends. Her friend had asked her parents to take Fran in and the State Agency agreed. It was the most normal family life Fran ever knew, but it only lasted one year. For the last three years of high school she lived with a school teacher and earned her keep by caring for her three children after school, in the evenings and on weekends.

So at a very early age she became her own support. While her peers were thinking about parties, boyfriends and having a good time, Fran had little time for anything but school and work. She must have inherited her father's strong work ethic, because from that point on, she supported herself and diligently worked hard at everything she did.

She earned her high school diploma and moved to Chicago, where she found a secretarial job. Soon she was able to live in a nice neighborhood and establish a normal lifestyle. But she was never able to put the guilt behind her. In fact, she felt more guilty than ever about splitting up her family, but she buried it in hard work and activity.

THE ONSLAUGHT OF DEPRESSION

Fran learned to make evasive answers about her family and at times lie about their whereabouts. When asked about holiday celebrations, she would insist that she was going to be with her family, and she would leave town to give such an appearance. She kept all the guilt and shame inside of her, and the deeper it went, the more depressed she became. Life seemed meaningless and dreary. Her strong work ethic kept her going, but there was no joy or happiness in her life.

She did make a few friends and began attending a church, though she had rarely attended any church while growing up. She wanted to be like everyone else, so she did anything she could to cover up her past and bury the guilt and the anger. No one knew the turmoil and pain inside of her. She did not dare let people know about her past for fear they would reject her and that she would be totally alone again.

DIVINE INTERVENTION

With depression as her constant companion, Fran could not help noticing the contrast she saw in the man she worked for. Dave Saulnier had a bubbly personality and seemed to be in a good mood all the time. She was not sure what it was that made him different, but Fran knew that he had something she did not have.

Opening the office mail one day, she began leafing through a newsletter entitled *Pacific Garden Mission News*. She had no idea what Pacific Garden was, but she noticed a story about Harry Saulnier, superintendent of the mission. When she inquired of her boss if there was any connection, he laughed and said, 'Yes, we're related. Harry Saulnier is my dad.' It turned out to be a divine intervention that had a great impact for good in Fran's life.

Several days later, with her heart heavy from depression, Fran discovered that Pacific Garden Mission was down the street from her office. Her searching heart was looking for any straw she could grasp as she felt herself overwhelmed with life. So she decided to go in and meet Dave's father.

By another divine intervention. Harry Saulnier was out of town, but his secretary, Helen Koester, took Fran on a tour of the mission. Since Fran had always tried to be good and do good things for others, she was impressed to see how the mission helped homeless and hungry people. But Helen wanted to show her a lot more than the mission, so over a cup of coffee, she explained to Fran that their main concern at the mission was the eternal souls of the people that came in their door.

A NEW BEGINNING

As the conversation continued, Helen began to share the truth of the Gospel with Fran. At first Fran was uncomfortable with the direction of the conversation and skeptical, but when Helen began to talk about forgiveness, that caught her attention. The load of guilt she had carried since she was twelve years old had become almost unbearable, and the idea that she could be forgiven overcame her reluctance to listen to Helen.

'What about something I've felt guilty about for years?' she asked Helen. Helen told her the good news that even though she had come short of God's requirements, by trusting in Christ anyone could be forgiven. Then she asked Fran a simple, direct question: 'Want to be free of guilt?'

No other words could have touched Fran as deeply as those. She could no longer hold back the tears, as she replied, 'After all these years? Oh, yes!' Helen prayed with her and, in simple faith, Fran asked for forgiveness and received Jesus into her life. Amazingly, as she walked out of the mission that afternoon, Fran knew that her heavy load of guilt was gone.

RECONCILIATION

Three months after her momentous decision, in June 1970, Fran went back to visit her mother, whom she had not seen since her father's funeral. As a Christian, she felt it was necessary for her to try to reconcile with her mother, but in her heart she was still fighting the anger and shame her mother had brought on her. In her mind she had a picture of her mother as a young woman, but what she saw was a forlorn, sick, shriveled-up woman living in even worse conditions than when the family had been together. She was virtually a stranger to Fran, and at this point Fran was not ready to forgive this person for what she had done, or to accept her into her life. She did not want to accept her as her mother or call her mother, and though she was civil to her, she was neither warm nor caring. She avoided any physical contact whatsoever with her.

Fran returned to Chicago with a heavy heart, feeling guilty again because she did not want to be reunited with her mother. She knew that she was supposed to forgive her mother, as she had been forgiven by Jesus, but it seemed like mission impossible. She felt that someday she would go back and tell her mother about the love of God and what He could do for her. But before that could happen, Fran's heart attitude toward her mother had to be changed.

THE FREEDOM OF FORGIVENESS

About a year later, in February 1971, Fran learned that her mother was very ill with cancer, so she went to see her on Valentine's Day of that year. She decided she must share her faith in Christ with her mother before the cancer killed her, and she determined to do so on this trip. She did not feel forgiving, but she decided to act in faith. She asked her good friend Beth to go with her.

They took Fran's mother to a nice restaurant for dinner, and though Fran felt burdened for her, she still had a wall built up in her heart to avoid any real closeness with her. It was probably a protective mechanism in her human nature that said, 'She hurt you before; don't get close enough to let her hurt you again.'

Trying to keep the conversation going, Fran asked how her mother had met her dad, and that led to other questions. Finally Fran asked, 'Have you ever been back to the cemetery to visit Dad's grave?' When she said she hadn't, Beth asked, 'Would you like to go there now?'

Her mother wanted to do that, and she remembered where the cemetery was located. Beth and Fran had to wander around the icy grounds of the cemetery for a while before they found the grave. Then they returned to the car to get Fran's mom and bring her there, and Beth decided to let Fran and her mother make that journey alone.

On the way to the grave, her mother stumbled and fell, and Fran was forced to touch her and help her up. She had been so careful to avoid any touch until this moment, but while she was helping her mother, it was as though the dam burst within her. Once she touched her, God's forgiveness flooded her mind and heart, and for the first time, she really wanted to forgive her mother.

As they walked on to the grave site, Fran held her mother by the arm and she thought, *Here we are alone in the cemetery. What better place for a person to wonder about her soul!* So she began what she had promised God she would do. 'Mom,' she said, 'did you ever stop to think about what's going to happen to your soul when you die? Would you like to go to heaven with me, Mom?' she asked.

Her mother looked at her and said yes, she wanted to go to heaven. Fran prayed with her mother to accept Christ into her life, but Fran was changed as well. She truly forgave her mother and loved her with the love of Christ. The heavy load of guilt and shame was forever lifted off her shoulders.

THE AFTERMATH OF RECONCILIATION

Once Fran had made peace with her mother and shared the Gospel with her, Fran's life started to come together in remarkable ways.

71

The collection business she had struggled to begin in 1969 was finally born full-time in 1973, and her dream of being a business owner came true. But it was more than a way to earn a living; her business became an avenue for witnessing.

Fran had two tracts written especially for her business. To collect a bill, she sent a tract and a kind, non-threatening letter. With each letter she mailed, Fran prayed that the Lord would use the letter and the tract to reach these people, and she left the results in the hands of the Lord.

Once people paid their debts, Fran would often take the opportunity to encourage them to think about the debt Christ paid for them. She would send out a thank-you tract containing the Gospel and a reply card offering additional information. Fran wanted to find a way to tell others about God's love and forgiveness since it had so transformed her life.

THE FAMILY REUNITED

When her mother was dying in 1972, Fran went to be at her side and was with her to the end. At that time her sister-in-law told Fran, 'You know, Mom said, "I'm so glad Frances came back and told me about the Lord".' What a wonderful gift for Fran to know that her mother had become a witness too, and that same sister-in-law became a believer as a result.

Fran was eventually able to share the Gospel with her older sister, who also was born from above. One by one, Fran has been in touch with every member of her family, traveling all over the country until she found all of them after much research. All but one of the siblings was reunited with their mother before her death. Fran's prayer now is that they will all be united again in heaven.

God used Fran even as a child to end the abuse in her family, even though, sadly, it also caused the breakup of her family. But in His incredible grace, He has turned the pain of a lifetime into a bouquet of beauty, as Fran has allowed God to heal her and make her an instrument of healing for her family. No wonder we call it 'Marvelous Grace.'

8

BATHSHEBA'S STORY

Bathsheba agreed to a liaison with a man who was not her husband, and it brought her shame and infamy which she could never have imagined, but she is certainly not the only woman to fall into that trap. I never cease to be amazed at the things we women will do to try to get a man or please a man. Why? Well, if you want my opinion, I think it goes back to the curse God placed upon Eve – and all of us in turn – in the Garden of Eden. You'll find that story recorded in Genesis 3. In verse 16 we see Eve's curse:

> To the woman He said, 'I will greatly increase your pains in childbearing; with pain you will give birth to children. Your desire will be for your husband, and he will rule over you.'

EVE'S CURSE PASSED DOWN
If you have ever given birth to a baby, you know only too well how effective this curse has been. In the midst of giving birth to a baby, most every woman wonders what made her ever think she wanted a baby, and vows never to let this happen again! Thankfully those pains are usually forgotten very quickly.

Do you realize that God intended for childbirth to be painless, but that because of the curse we must now endure that pain? It is a reminder to each of us women who have given birth – a very personal reminder – of our mother Eve's transgression and its resultant effects in our lives!

But the other part of that curse given to Eve had to do with her relationship to men, in particular her desire for her man. We can only imagine what the marriage relationship would have been like without the curse, but you can be sure that God intended for it to be a very harmonious, equal relationship, without all these control issues, submission issues and abuse issues that are the trademark of many relationships today. That was not God's intention for marriage; it happened as a result of sin entering into that relationship.

Thankfully, when two people bring God back into their marriage as the controlling person, they can enjoy a marriage relationship that bears a close resemblance to what God originally intended for marriage.

This desire to have a man is so strong within us women that we are willing to endure all kinds of mistreatment just to have that man – that one man we can call ours. This sin-induced curse makes normally intelligent, sane women do dumb, often insane things, and behave in the most ridiculous ways over some man. Unfortunately, I speak from experience!

BATHSHEBA'S FALL

Bathsheba made a fool of herself over a man, and she allowed that man to so control her that she almost ruined her life completely (the story is found in 2 Sam. 11). Now I admit that Bathsheba found herself in a very difficult situation. It was no ordinary man she was dealing with; it was King David. Granted that would give any woman pause, especially since David was undoubtedly mega-attractive.

Women today make similar mistakes with men. A man with power, prestige, money and looks, or any one of these, can cause us to abandon our principles, forget our commitments, and make ourselves totally vulnerable. Many women are intimidated by this type of man. After all, how do you refuse a 'king'? Well, you refuse a 'king' the way you do any other man; it is really quite simple. But we often lose our ability to reason when we encounter the man of fame and power.

You could feel sorry for Bathsheba, I suppose. All she was doing was taking a bath and the next thing she knows, she is in hot water! How could she know that King David would be watching from the adjoining rooftop?

Or then again, how could she not know? Was she unaware that the king lived nearby and could view her rooftop from his? I doubt she was that naive or unaware. Do you think she might have intended to flaunt her beauty, perhaps even teasing the king a bit? Certainly we women have been known to flirt. Many times we like the fun of flirting, even though we never intend for it to go further. But we should always be aware that flirting can lead to inappropriate encounters, and it is not something to mess around with.

Whether intentionally or not, Bathsheba was observed while she bathed by a lustful King David. Not accustomed to being denied anything he desired, David called for Bathsheba to come to his parlor. That was step one toward trouble – big trouble. At this point either one of these two adults could have, and should have, made a conscious decision to do the right thing.

DAVID'S SIN

David knew God well; he knew God's law well, and he knew this was wrong, sinful and selfish of him. Why did he do what he knew was wrong?

Well, we can guess. Perhaps he saw himself as above the law. Many times when people find themselves in positions of power and authority, the status goes to their heads, and they think the rules are not for them but for everyone else. Certainly King David had known his share of praise and adoration. Maybe David had not been reading the law much lately. After all, he was a busy man. It would be understandable if he had to postpone his time with God and the law. Perhaps, then, the problem was that God's law just was not uppermost on his mind. Doing God's will was not his highest priority at that moment because he had neglected God's Word.

I can relate to that. When I think I am too busy to spend time with God, I know how fast I slide down that slippery slope. Things we would never dream of doing when the lines are open between us and the Lord seem less sinful, less prohibited when we aren't immersed in God's Word.

David may have innocently and unintentionally observed Bathsheba at first. His mistake was that he did not remove himself immediately from the temptation. One quick glimpse would have told him that he should not be watching another man's wife taking a bath. But David kept watching until the lust of his eyes led him to take action.

'What is the harm in watching?' he might have said. 'As long as I just look, why, who could object?' Isn't it amazing how easily we rationalize what we want to do? David well knew that this was a point of temptation for him and that he was very vulnerable to this type of sin. No doubt he was a virile man, the type we women swoon over, and he had a history of going after women. Even though it was somewhat acceptable in the culture of that day, it was not acceptable to God. The law on adultery was clear and David knew it. No excuses, David!

When we linger long in the territory of temptation, we invite disaster. When we rationalize sinful behavior, we take that first step, which makes all the other downward steps easier and faster. It is the first step into sin that we must avoid.

David's son, Solomon, would later give us very good advice about temptation:

> Let your eyes look straight ahead, fix your gaze directly before you. Make level paths for your feet and take only ways that are firm. Do not swerve to the right or the left; keep your foot from evil (Prov. 4:25–27).

I wonder if late in life, knowing the terrible outcome of his sin, David sat down with Solomon and taught him these proverbs – these wise sayings. Unfortunately, Solomon also failed to take his own advice, and we know the sad story of his addiction to women.

If David had fixed his gaze in the right direction when he was on the rooftop that fateful evening, he could have avoided his lustful desire for Bathsheba. But he failed to keep his foot from evil. I look at my own life and realize that those times of getting off the beaten path began with that first step. After that, it is a fast decline.

I continually ask God to help me focus on not taking that first step in the wrong direction – that is the only way I can be certain that I stay on the right path. None of us are above any temptation, and the temptations of the flesh and sexual desire are unbelievably strong. They are also the sins that cause the most heartache and sorrow.

BATHSHEBA'S SIN

On the other hand, Bathsheba could not have been ignorant of what she was doing when she accepted David's invitation. Was she intimidated by his authority? Or could she have been immensely flattered by his attention? Had she given it some thought, Bathsheba might have realized that all David was after was her body. He had never had a conversation with her as far as we know. The attraction was physical.

Now, don't get me wrong, I would love to have a great body, but many times I have thanked God that He spared me from that struggle. There is no doubt that great bodies turn the heads of men; they are visual creatures and their eyes often lead them astray. If you are a woman with a very attractive body and shape, be aware of your responsibility to keep from flaunting it. Certainly that does not excuse any man's behavior, but some women love to stir up the flame.

How flattering can it be to know that someone is attracted to your body only? Shouldn't Bathsheba have seen David's invitation as an insult, not to mention evil? David had no intention of anything more than having a fling. Had Bathsheba not gotten pregnant it is unlikely he ever would have married her.

Interestingly, David was not a bum. He was a man after God's own heart, yet he led Bathsheba astray. I have noticed that when we are tempted by a good man, we try to rationalize it by saying, 'But he is not that type of man; he really loves me,' or some other such nonsense. My answer to that is, 'So what?'

A young, attractive woman was telling me about a relationship she was having with a man who was more than willing to take advantage of her company and occupy all her time, but not willing to make any commitment. Sound familiar? She told me over and over what a good person he is and how everybody likes him. I tried to gently point out that obviously something was wrong with his sense of honor because of the way he was treating her. He was willing to keep her occupied and unavailable to anyone else, even though he had no intentions of a permanent relationship, knowing all along that she was secretly hoping the relationship would develop further.

That is quite selfish and dishonest, if you ask me. He was not quite the knight in shining armor that she described. After all, it was no bad thing for his ego to know that an attractive woman was hanging on for dear life, hoping for something more. That had to give him good feelings, so why should he stop as long as she was willing to put up with him? She rationalized her own foolish behavior because he was 'so nice,' hanging onto an unrealistic hope that someday, miraculously, he would see the light and realize what a jewel he had in her.

Maybe Bathsheba was fooled by the same type of thinking. David was such a good man, a godly man. She could trust him. He would never harm her intentionally. But at that moment in time, David was controlled by his hormones, and he did exactly that.

So Bathsheba, for whatever reason, accepted David's invitation. She did his bidding and suffered the consequences – an unwanted pregnancy. All for that one night of pleasure; all because one man had shown her some attention and she had fallen under his spell; all because she was unwilling to say 'no'.

Why is it that we women will let a man take advantage of us like this, even when we know his feelings are shallow and selfish? Back to the curse, if you ask me. I have had many a woman tell me about the power some man has over her, all the time recognizing that he is using her and does not really care for her. Yet she hangs on for dear life! Sensible, sane women would not behave like that. It has to be this sin-induced curse that we have had to bear since the beginning of time.

SET FREE FROM THE CURSE

Oh, but the great news is, Jesus came to set us free from the curse! Galatians 3:13 tells us: 'Christ redeemed us from the curse of the law by becoming a curse for us, for it is written: "Cursed is everyone who is hung on a tree."' Women today who have been redeemed by Christ no longer have to endure this curse. Jesus became a curse for us (this is really difficult for my mind to comprehend) so that I no longer have to be a slave to the curse of the law.

Curses are terrible things to be avoided, yet Jesus voluntarily became a curse for you and me. Why? Because God's holiness demanded justice, and the perfect sacrifice had to become sin to satisfy the demands of the law. That curse God pronounced in the Garden could not simply be dropped; it had to be brought to fruition. Hence, Jesus became the curse in our place.

No more excuses. I do not have to be under the power of that curse. I do not have to be controlled by an uncontrollable desire for a man, Jesus came to set me free from that curse. If any of us who are born from above choose to remain under this curse, it is because we either are not willing or don't know how to appropriate the victory we have because of Jesus.

Let me add that being free from the curse does not mean we are free from our desires to be married and have children. Nor would we want to be! And it certainly does not mean we are free from the commitments we make to our mates; quite the opposite. But it does mean we can be free from the addiction to men so many of us have experienced, an addiction which usually results in bad choices and ruined relationships!

GRACE FOR BATHSHEBA

Bathsheba had to endure the killing of her good and loyal husband, and eventually the death of the baby. She must have been a crushed woman. True, David married her and she lived her life out with him, having other children by him, but I wonder how many times she thought, 'If only I hadn't gone when David asked for me.... If only I had been faithful to my husband. If only....'

Would you have chosen Bathsheba to be a fore-mother of the Messiah? If the Messiah had to come through David's line, why not through Abigail? She was such a special woman of honor and duty, and David had married her years before the incident with Bathsheba. But it was through Bathsheba's son, Solomon, that the birth of Jesus took place.

There is that incredible grace again.

Every time I tell and retell these stories, I literally shake my head and marvel at God's grace. How infinitely patient and forgiving He is with us sinners. With all that Bathsheba did wrong, with all the disgrace and sorrow she brought on herself and her family, she is still allowed this select role in the birth of Jesus, and Matthew chose to list her in the genealogy of Matthew 1.

THERE'S HOPE FOR US ALL

Is adultery a part of your past or some other sexual sin? If so, you will have already paid a high price for that sin no doubt. Whether it is a deep, dark secret that you have been keeping inside of you, or whether it has been exposed for all the world to see, perhaps with the birth of a baby, the disgrace may haunt you. You probably feel dirty. You may wonder if anyone will ever want you again, especially God.

Bathsheba's story reminds us that God still uses broken and marred vessels. God can qualify people for service even though other humans – even His own children – may try to put them on the shelf. I am often amazed to see how quickly the Christian community is ready to disqualify someone from service. Often we have our own versions of the scarlet letter, which we drape around certain people who have committed certain wrongs. Oh, it is an invisible scarlet letter, but nonetheless well known throughout our fellowships.

Do not misunderstand – we need standards and high principles of conduct for any who would serve in our churches or Christian organizations. But we do not need unbiblical litmus tests which represent / regard certain sins and transgressions as unforgivable.

Romans 8:1 tells us that there is no condemnation for those who are in Christ Jesus, and I believe God meant exactly what the Apostle Paul penned. No condemnation – none for nobody for no reason! God does not have scarlet letters of condemnation. He has grace and forgiveness for those who come to Him with a repentant heart.

Yes, there is hope for you. God specializes in rehabilitation and restoration, and He loves to demonstrate what His grace can do with a person who has made a terrible mess out of her life.

That is the story of Bathsheba – it is the story of God's grace to an undeserving woman who made a fool of herself over a man. God restored her and gave her a most important role to play: grandmother (many times removed) of His Son, the Messiah.

Like Bathsheba, my friend Judy discovered the pain of being involved with a married man. After many years of confusion, her seeking heart led her to a place where she learned about Jesus.

9

JUDY'S STORY

Like Bathsheba, Judy has had to live with the consequences of her past, and it has caused her years of isolation and rejection.

A good word to describe Judy is bouncy. She always seems to have plenty of enthusiasm, a good attitude, a helpful spirit and a servant heart. However, I now know her well enough to realize that her life has not been easy. She has gone through many troubles, and underneath the smile are a lot of regrets. She would tell you that she is having to live with some of the poor choices and decisions she made in her younger years, and she is resigned to the fact that she will always have to face those unhappy facts.

The grace of God is evident in Judy's life; the bouncy Judy is not a facade. She is enthusiastic about life, she has a great attitude in spite of some unpleasant circumstances, and she always seems to be reaching out to other people with a helping hand and a compassionate heart. Many times she has called our office to ask us to pray for someone else; someone who has a heavy burden that Judy is sharing. She is a woman transformed by God's astonishing grace.

EARLY PATTERNS

Like so many other people, Judy grew up in a family that was religious only on the holidays. She heard that Jesus was the Son of God and that He died for our sins. One Easter season she remembers her mother making her sit in silence on Good Friday because that was when Jesus had hung on the cross. It stands out in her mind because it was such an unusual thing for religion even to be mentioned at home.

As a young girl, some friends invited her to Awana meetings at a local church, and she found that enjoyable. Five years later she was confirmed in another church, though she had no idea that this was supposed to be a life-changing commitment. Church was just a nice social place to go; she enjoyed singing in the choir and being with her friends.

That is until she discovered boys in her teenage years. She started going out in her early teens, and her idea of a double date was to come home early from one date and turn around and go back out with another boy. She had no difficulty attracting the boys, and she loved the attention. One, however, just was not enough for her.

At the age of seventeen she became engaged. It was exciting to wear the ring the boy gave her, but when she found out that he had been drafted into the military service, she realized he would be leaving her alone for a long time. Judy was able to convince him that it would be good for her to go out with some other men while he was away. She liked being engaged, but she was not ready to give up her freedom. There were just too many other guys out there to ignore!

Looking for Gusto

With her fiancé away, she did continue to see other men. Soon the dazzle from that ring wore off, and she knew she was not ready to be confined to just one man. So, when he was back home on furlough, she gave his ring back and regained her 'freedom.' It was painful for him, but for Judy, life was still a lark, and she wanted to sow her wild oats and make sure she partook of every excitement possible.

In her quest for the 'gusto,' she found herself involved with a married man. It seemed exciting at first – the thrill of forbidden fruit. He had four children, and he found Judy a welcome respite from his home responsibilities. He was more than willing to continue seeing her, though he offered her no future and no commitment.

Judy hung on for dear life, thinking he really cared for her, dreaming that somehow he would be hers someday. She held on to this dream through seven long years, hoping against hope that he would divorce his wife and marry her. These were not seven blissful years. They were instead stolen moments with her lover, filled with broken promises, nights of waiting, drunken visits, excuses, apologies, and more of the same in unending cycles. He was intensely jealous of Judy and often accused her of fooling around with other men, which she never did. Of course, all this time he was returning home to his family after his escapades with Judy and carrying on his relationship with his wife, but he wanted Judy to be his alone. Like so many women before her, since the beginning of time, Judy endured this miserable double standard because she thought she could not live without him.

There were many unpleasant encounters during this long affair, with family and friends trying to make Judy see the foolishness of hanging on to this married man. Even his wife begged her to break off the relationship, when she learned of it. But Judy's lover was able to persuade her that they could not live without each other, and so for seven long years Judy bought into that lie. Finally, when he became physically abusive toward her, she found the strength to end the relationship.

ALWAYS RESTLESS

After this long, frustrating affair, Judy felt she was very lucky when just a few months later she met a really nice man who wanted to marry her. The excitement was not there, but it was a safe relationship. Judy felt he could never hurt her in the way the other man had. She was grateful to have a normal relationship and felt that life was at last taking a turn for the better.

But her restless, wandering heart came back to haunt her. After three and a half good years in her marriage, she felt something was missing. Once again she started down that slippery slope of looking for 'excitement and thrills' in her life. She even began some counseling to try to help her find herself.

This was a puzzle and a mystery to her good and dependable husband. He had no idea why Judy was unhappy in the relationship, and he did not know what more he could do to meet her needs. Eventually, Judy's search for that missing piece led her into another affair with a long-time friend who was also the brother of her best friend. He was a 'take-charge' type of person, and she felt that, unlike the other men in her life, he would take care of her. It was wishful thinking on her part; he never pretended to love her. Perhaps it was the challenge of trying to reach him when he appeared unreachable that sucked Judy in. She tried desperately to make him love her, but she always knew that he never did.

With that affair, her marriage came to an end, and she was separated from her husband.

TRYING TO GET CONTROL

While waiting for her divorce to become final, continuing her on-again, off-again affair with this long-time friend, Judy became pregnant. This was definitely not something she had considered, and she was in a quandary. She could not tell her family; they were already very angry with her for leaving her husband and had almost disowned her for it. Since she knew that her lover did not really love her, she could not imagine that he would want their baby. There was a possibility that he would have done the 'honorable thing' and married Judy, but she could not bear the thought of his marrying her only because of the baby, so she discounted that option. In addition, she was working two jobs just to support herself. How could she afford a baby?

Judy figured that maybe her counselor could offer some help. As she described the panic she was feeling, her psychiatrist urged her to get control of her life. His advice was to abort the baby and start over. She did not really want to do that because one of her lifelong dreams had been to have a baby. However, she felt she was in this mess all by herself and that she had to try to get some control of her life.

In that time of confusion and emotional upheaval, Judy decided to take the psychiatrist's advice, and she aborted her baby. She hardly had time to consider her actions, it all happened so quickly. She remembers how the reality of what she had done began to dawn on her when she was taken into the recovery room after the abortion. Why did she have to throw away the only thing she ever really wanted in life – a baby of her own? No one told her about the aftermath of abortion. No one explained the many options she had. No one urged her to save the precious life inside of her. The only advice she received was to 'get control' of her life through abortion.

Of course, it had just the opposite effect on Judy. Life became even more chaotic. It was Christmastime, and she found herself all alone. The abortion had left her feeling desolate, and with the holidays, that loneliness increased. When she discovered that her family had invited her ex-husband to the family Christmas Eve gathering but had not invited her, she began to realize how isolated and alone she really was.

After Christmas things got worse. She decided she would never tell her lover about the baby and the abortion, but somehow he guessed. When he asked her if she was pregnant and she told him the truth, his reaction surprised her. He was angry and hurt. 'You could have had the baby and given it to me,' was his response, and with that he ended their relationship, such as it was. When Judy realized that he had wanted the baby but not her, she was even more devastated.

On top of all that, her best friend found out about Judy's affair with her brother. She knew that Judy had left a good husband, a man she liked very much, and thrown away her marriage for this affair. She could not find it in her heart to forgive Judy. So Judy lost her marriage, her baby, her lover and her best friend, all within a few short months.

But the worst thing was the torment that began to plague her day and night, the guilt of killing her baby. It grew worse with time as she would think, *my baby would be two months old now* or *my baby would be walking by now*. She could not forgive herself. Judy had not gained control of her life; instead, everything was spinning totally out of control.

BOTTOMING OUT

The next three years of her life are a blur in Judy's mind. In order to avoid thinking about what she had done, in order to stay out of trouble, in order to survive, she continued to work two jobs. She was filled with deep regret for the baby she had thrown away, the baby that now could be growing and giving her joy. She was disappointed with her lover for not loving her. She tried to convince herself that her problems were all because of other people, but of course she knew better.

Days passed into weeks, weeks into months. Life was dark and dreary. Christmas of 1983 found Judy alone again. It was a very cold winter in Chicago, and her apartment was extremely drafty. The few ornaments she had put on her Christmas tree would swing in the breeze from the wind blowing in through cracks around her windows. Their clanging and tinkling could be heard throughout her apartment, especially when the wind was strong, as it so often is in the Windy City.

On Christmas morning, waking up in that very cold 40-degree apartment, Judy was physically sick and mentally confused. She heard someone swearing in her apartment. Who was it? Who woke her up with such profanity? With a raging fever and a broken heart, Judy finally realized she had been listening to herself. She was the one spewing out that barrage of cursing and perversion. Who was this person she had become? In that painful moment, Judy got a glimpse of what was happening to her. It was like a cold slap in her face, a wake-up call. She was at the lowest ebb of her life.

Through all the hard years, Judy had always thought that even if everyone else failed her, she could count on herself and that would be enough. She had refused to recognize her dire situation, pretending even to herself that she could take care of things. She was tough. But on that cold Christmas morning, she knew that she had been telling herself a lie. She could not take care of herself. For the first time she admitted that she had lost control of her life and made a total mess of it. The emptiness inside of her could no longer be denied.

At the bottom on that day, it dawned on her that she had not given any thought to the meaning of Christmas that year. What was the real meaning of it anyway? Her thoughts began to turn to that God she had heard about as a child. Was He there? Could He – would He – help her?

THE ROAD BACK UP

Two weeks after Christmas, Judy decided to attend a church nearby to see a movie about Joni Eareckson. She had read her story in *People* magazine and was intrigued by her battle with paralysis after her diving accident. She thought it would be interesting to hear how she was coping with life in a wheelchair, so in curiosity, she wandered alone into the church that evening.

To her surprise, the church was packed with people. She had never seen so many people in a church, and wondered if it was just for the movie or if they came to the regular services in large numbers too. The movie about Joni certainly was interesting, but she did not realize it would be so 'religious.'

Out of curiosity she went back to the church the following week to see if all those people would be there on Sunday and, to her surprise, they were. This really intrigued her. Why would so many people give up their day off on Sunday to come to this church? She wanted to know why, so she decided to attend some classes that were offered for those who were seekers.

Having sung in a choir previously, she particularly watched the choir in this church. She had never seen a church choir like this one. They really seemed to believe what they were singing. They were not just trying to make music, they were singing about something that had made a difference in their lives. Judy knew they had something she did not have, and she began to want it.

SET FREE BY THE TRUTH

Judy got to know one of the choir members and asked her why this choir seemed so different. She explained to Judy that each member of the choir had a personal relationship with Jesus. That was a new language to Judy. She knew that Jesus had died for the sins of the world, so she thought that included her sins, but she could never remember hearing anyone talk about having a personal relationship with Jesus. She continued to be drawn to these church services, and a month and a half after that first visit, as she sat alone in the Sunday service, the pastor invited people who needed Christ in their lives to come to the front of the church. Judy did not intend to respond to that invitation; it seemed strange to her. Yet, as the pastor continued to make the invitation, Judy found herself drawn to the front of the church, almost as if in a dream. A woman from the church took her aside and made plans to meet with Judy at her home for a Bible study. Judy met with this woman one-on-one a few times, and on March 28, 1984, while Judy was praying with this woman, she accepted the gift of salvation offered by Jesus, gave Him control of her life, and painstakingly confessed each of her sins to the Lord one by one, asking for His forgiveness. She knew that she was indeed forgiven.

She did not know what to expect, but it was life-changing. The burden of guilt that had plagued her for years seemed to drop off, right there that day. She understood the term 'born again' – that is exactly the way she felt, as if she had been born all over again, with a whole new life before her. She was free from the sins of her past, free from the guilt, free from the bitterness and anger. Truly and finally free.

GROWING IN GRACE

The years since have been an adventure in faith for Judy. She tells of the marvelous changes in her life:

Now when I sing hymns like 'Amazing Grace,' it really means something to me. Psalm 86:13 reads: 'For great is your love toward me; you have delivered me from the depths of the grave.' Before I came to Jesus I was plagued with nightmares, the kind that wake you in a sweat with your heart pounding. There was always someone (unknown) chasing me. As hard and as fast as I ran, I could never get away; and I always woke up just at the point of being caught. I believe that it was Satan in my dreams and that is how close I came to giving myself up to him. I was playing in his territory and having a grand time, until my world came crashing down on me, and the reality of my sinfulness and my need for the Savior broke through.

Judy has had to deal with the baggage of her past; and it still causes her shame. The child she threw away in a moment of weakness, panic and selfishness is lost to her forever in this life. Forgiving herself for this has not been easy. She knew the Lord had forgiven her when she accepted Christ, but it took three years to learn to forgive herself.

In a wonderful way, God removed this burden of guilt from Judy one Sunday when, as a volunteer at her church, she was asked to collect all the attendance reports from the Sunday school classes. For some reason, when she reached the nursery, the regular attendants were not there; and a mother was there to leave her baby. Assuming Judy was the nursery attendant, she thrust the baby into her arms and walked off to her class before Judy could object or explain.

Judy sat down in a rocker and spent an hour holding and rocking that little one, and she could feel the healing touch of God in her own life that morning. God used that incident to set her free from the excruciating pain and guilt of her abortion. After that, she volunteered to work in the nursery and now loves to be around babies whenever possible.

Judy also knew she needed to seek the forgiveness of her ex-husband. She had no idea what his reaction would be, but it had to be done. She found he was very ready to forgive her, and she had the opportunity to tell him about the incredible change in her life.

REACHING OUT TO OTHERS

At the time she accepted Christ, Judy was working for *Playboy* magazine, in the accounting department. She began to realize that she needed to change her place of employment, but before she left God had some work for her to do there. She had the joy of seeing four of her co-workers ask Christ into their lives and another recommit her life to Him, right in that most unlikely place. She now works for another organization and continues to tell the good news about life in Christ.

The years since that pivotal day in March 1984 have brought ups and downs, but Judy insists that following Jesus is a decision she has never regretted, not for a moment. 'He gives my life peace and meaning,' she says. 'Each day is an adventure. When I give each one to Him, I never know who or what He will bring into it, but I know I can trust Him and follow Him, wherever He leads me.'

Because of the pain and sorrow she has known, Judy is able to empathize with and love others who are in pain. It seems that God brings many of those kinds of people into her life, and in that way He is using even her shameful past to bring glory to Himself.

Truly the God of grace has salvaged Judy's life from the depths of sin and given her new hope, new joy, new meaning and something to really live for. Not all of her dreams will come true in this life, and she will never be able to escape some of the consequences of her past, but through all of it, her Lord is there to comfort, to encourage without condemnation, and to make something beautiful out of the ashes of her life. It is more than just love; more than just forgiveness; more even than just mercy. It is grace. Astonishing grace.

10

MARY OF NAZARETH'S STORY

Mary never had a halo. She was not divine. She was a woman like you and me, chosen for the most important female role in history. So while it is not biblical or accurate to elevate her to a place of deity and worship, it is also not right to overlook her place in history and in God's plan. This was a very special woman – the most blessed woman who ever lived. Yet I am sure she would have been the first to tell us that her life's story was one of God's transforming grace.

BORN IN THE WRONG PLACE

Nazareth was not the right side of the railroad tracks back in the days when Jesus was born. People didn't proudly stand up and say, 'I'm from Nazareth.' If that happened to be your lot in life, you tried to keep it quiet. To be a Nazarene indicated you were likely poor, uneducated, unsophisticated, perhaps even unethical. 'Can anything good come out of Nazareth?' people used to say (John 1:46).

To prove His transforming power, to show how God 'chose the weak things of the world to shame the strong ... the lowly things of this world and the despised things – and the things that are not – to nullify the things that are' (1 Cor. 1:27-28), God chose a very humble, young woman from Nazareth for the most important assignment He had ever given or ever would give to any woman.

BORN IN POVERTY

Coming from a very humble family, poor by the world's definition, probably uneducated and unsophisticated by worldly standards, Mary fit the Nazarene stereotype, apart from the 'unethical' or 'bad' stigma that was attached to those from Nazareth. In spite of its poverty and lack of social status, Mary's family was undoubtedly strong and God-fearing. We are given no details of her parents or her childhood, but there are many clues that indicate she had a godly upbringing.

She must have had a good knowledge of Scripture. In Luke 1:46-55 we find Mary's song, or what has often been referred to as 'Mary's Magnificat.' It is the beautiful, poetic response from Mary's heart when her cousin Elizabeth recognizes and hails her as the blessed woman she is. There are many phrases and words in Mary's song that come directly from various Psalms. This Magnificat reflects her knowledge of the prophets Isaiah and Jeremiah, and it is clear that she knew about Abraham and his descendants, and of God's promise to her people.

HOME SCHOOLED

Where did Mary get her education? It would be easier to explain if she had been a man, because men were taught in the synagogues, but being a woman, how did she develop such an intimate knowledge of Old Testament Scripture? The most reasonable explanation is that she was home-schooled. Her parents taught her; she heard the scriptures discussed around the dinner table and she saw it lived in their lives.

Mary's song tells me that this young woman had heard those Psalms sung many times, so that she knew them by heart. She had also heard the stories of Abraham, Isaac and Jacob. She knew that she was born in the line of King David. Her home-schooling had given her a foundation of knowledge and faith unlike that of most women of her day. Mary came from ordinary, even humble people, but she had a godly heritage that was more valuable than riches or position.

MARY'S CALLING

The Christmas story has been so romanticized through the years that it is hardly recognizable when you read it in the Bible. With the crèches, pageants and live manger scenes that are everywhere to be found, we have lost touch with the reality of this event.

To my mind the romantic part of this story comes at the very beginning, when a simple young girl receives a visit from the Number One Angel! Let's look at that passage in Luke 1:26-38:

> In the sixth month, God sent the angel Gabriel to Nazareth, a town in Galilee, to a virgin pledged to be married to a man named Joseph, a descendant of David. The virgin's name was Mary. The angel went to her and said, 'Greetings, you who are highly favored! The Lord is with you.' Mary was greatly troubled at his words and wondered what kind of greeting this might be. But the angel said to her, 'Do not be afraid, Mary; you have found favor with God. You will be with child and give birth to a son, and you are to give Him the name Jesus. He will be great and will be called the Son of the Most High. The Lord God will give Him the throne of His father David, and He will reign over the house of Jacob forever; His kingdom will never end.' 'How will this be,' Mary asked the angel, 'since I am a virgin?' The angel answered, 'The Holy Spirit will come upon you, and the power of the Most High will overshadow you. So the holy one to be born will be called the Son of God. Even Elizabeth your relative is going to have a child in her old age, and she who was said to be barren is in her sixth month. For nothing is impossible with God.'
>
> 'I am the Lord's servant,' Mary answered. 'May it be to me as you have said.' Then the angel left her.

Angel visits were not common, even back then. Put yourself into the shoes of this young girl, probably under eighteen years old, living in a very humble home, finding herself face-to-face with Gabriel. I imagine she was just doing her everyday things, thinking about her fiancé Joseph, planning her wedding, looking forward to being a wife and mother. She was expecting a normal Nazareth life.

Yes, she knew that someday one Jewish girl would be chosen to bear the Messiah. She had heard this all her life, and though she may have occasionally dreamed it would be her, undoubtedly she never really thought it could happen. And then she was face-to-face with an angel. Angels were known in Scripture to take different forms, so we really are not sure just what Gabriel looked like to Mary, but for sure, he was someone she had never seen or talked to before in her life. He simply appeared, and greeted her in a most unusual way.

MARY'S QUALIFICATIONS

We are told that it was Gabriel's words rather than his looks that troubled Mary (see Luke 1:26-38): 'Greetings, you who are highly favored! The Lord is with you.'

Mary must have wondered, *What kind of greeting is this?* She certainly didn't consider herself highly favored. How could she – a Nazarene, a hardworking girl from a poor family, marrying a hardworking carpenter – how could she be 'highly favored'?

'The Lord is with you.' What did that mean to Mary? Yes, she knew the God of her fathers, she knew His name was Jehovah, but He was God in heaven, God of her people. She probably had never thought of Him as the Lord who was with her, so Gabriel's greeting confused and frightened her.

Yet his next statement must have been the most beautiful words she had ever heard: 'Do not be afraid, Mary, you have found favor with God.' What an incredible thing! God approved of how she lived her life, He was pleased with her character, and He was putting His stamp of approval on her plans and relationships. She had found favor with God.

I have often dreamed of being the Mary who heard those words. I want to hear them someday. There have been a few occasions when I sensed His favor and knew that He was pleased, and there really is nothing to compare with the peace, the contentment, the inner 'high' that comes when you know you and God are absolutely in sync.

The good news is that we can achieve that status, just as Mary from Nazareth did, by obedience, by loving Jesus above all else, by staying close to Him throughout our days. We are easily distracted by the world around us, but if we could ever just get a taste of what it is like to 'find favor with God,' we would find it difficult to settle for anything less.

Mary found such favor with God that He allowed her to go through an experience that was going to break her heart, cause her untold grief, bring many moments of distress, ruin her reputation, and put her life in jeopardy. Makes you want to ask: What would God have done to her if she had not found favor with Him?

But we need to learn a lesson from this. When someone finds favor with God – when He sees a willing, obedient heart – He often gives that person tough assignments because He can trust him or her with those tough assignments. Not everyone is qualified or willing to do the hard things that must be done. While there was an unspeakable joy, which Mary carried in her heart all her days, the joy of being chosen for this most blessed duty, she surely was given a very difficult assignment.

MARY'S REACTION

As Gabriel continued his conversation with Mary, he informed her that she would give birth to the Son of the Most High, the One who would take the throne of His father David. Can you imagine what Gabriel's words meant to a Jewish girl who had heard all her life about David, his kingdom and his reign as King of Israel? Now she was being told that her son would take David's place and reign forever.

If you had been Mary, how would you have reacted? It was an incredible declaration, requiring enormous faith on Mary's part. Would you have accepted such a statement at face value? Notice how Mary reacted. She asked a very simple question, not a question of doubt, not a challenge to the truth of the angel's statement, but a question of curiosity and logic. To paraphrase, she asked: 'How will I have a baby, when I've never known a man? If you're not going to use an earthly man for this, how are you going to do it?'

To this simple, honest question, Gabriel gave a simple answer: 'The Holy Spirit will come upon you, and the power of the Most High will overshadow you. So the holy one to be born will be called the Son of God.'

Mary's acceptance of this announcement was absolutely remarkable. Once Gabriel answered her simple question, in the same simple faith and openness, she accepted: 'I am the Lord's servant. May it be to me as you have said.' Instead of plying Gabriel with hundreds of questions, instead of giving place to all the doubts, fears and insecurities that she must have felt at that time, Mary accepted.

Let us think of some of the normal, natural questions and objections that Mary could have legitimately raised at that point. She could have said:

- Gabriel, what will I tell my friends and relatives? No one will believe that I have not slept with some man. What will happen to my reputation?

- What will I tell Joseph? He probably won't want to marry me now.
- And if Joseph doesn't marry me, what will I do to support myself and this baby? I will be an outcast.
- Worse still, Gabriel, if Joseph so desires he could divorce me or he could have me stoned to death for adultery.
- Why don't you, Gabriel, just tell everyone else what you have told me? I would appreciate your doing that. Then maybe they will believe me. At least tell everyone in Nazareth, please.

Wouldn't you have asked some of these questions or made some other requests of Gabriel? Faced with a similar situation, I'm sure I would have.

But not this Mary. Her immediate, unquestioning response was, 'May it be to me as you have said.' Now we're beginning to see why God liked Mary so much. She had an accepting, unquestioning heart.

MARY'S READY FAITH

Mary believed with unwavering faith. Can you appreciate the enormity of what she was asked to accept by faith? She was asked to believe that she would become pregnant without ever having had relations with any man. And Mary believed.

Why do you think Mary so readily believed what Gabriel told her? Do you think it is possible to just have that kind of trust and faith without any preparation? Was she just born that way?

I do not think so. We know that faith comes by hearing, and hearing by the Word of God. We know from Mary's song that she knew the Word of God. She had established her faith in God's Word, so when Gabriel brought this further Word of God to her, she was accustomed to trusting it, and it was not difficult for her to trust it once more.

We are never going to be able to trust God like Mary of Nazareth until we spend consistent quality and quantity time in His Word. Are you in the midst of some testing now?

Are you under some stress or pressure that requires faith on your part? I hope you have been staying in the Word of God daily, because that is the source of faith. You need to know the Word of God to have the kind of trust that Mary had.

MARY'S VIRGINITY

Certainly Scripture makes it clear that Mary was then a virgin and remained a virgin until after the birth of Jesus. You know, not many people who celebrate Christmas really believe that Jesus was born of a virgin. Why is it so terribly important that we believe and accept that Mary was indeed a virgin until after Jesus' birth? It is because we know from Scripture that sin entered the world through the seed of man. Had Jesus been conceived through an earthly man's seed, He could not have escaped the sin-nature that is born into all of us. He could never have become the sacrifice demanded by God's righteousness. But Jesus Christ was perfect because there was no sin in Him passed on to Him by the seed of man. That is critical. The virgin birth is not optional theology; our eternal destiny depends upon whether or not it is true. We are acceptable to God when we accept the redemption and forgiveness of our sins made possible by the perfect sacrificial Lamb, Jesus Christ.

A SPIRITUAL COCOON

When the angel left her, Mary went to the one person with whom she could share the news, the one person she knew would understand, her cousin Elizabeth. Elizabeth was bearing a miracle baby, too – a child given to her in old age after years of infertility. Gabriel had told her about Elizabeth's soon-to-be-delivered baby, and I believe that he did so deliberately, so that Mary would realize she could go to her cousin's home for refuge. He must have known how much Mary would need Elizabeth in these early months of her pregnancy.

When Mary came into Elizabeth's presence, Elizabeth was filled with the Holy Spirit and immediately recognized Mary's condition even before Mary could tell her. Mary did not even have to form the words to tell Elizabeth what had happened to her; she did not have to go through a barrage of questions from Elizabeth. Instead, Elizabeth immediately started rejoicing with Mary.

That must have been such a relief to Mary! On the long trip from Nazareth to the hill country of Judea, she must have wondered how Elizabeth and Zechariah would respond to her and her news. What if they did not believe her? Where would she go then? So, when Elizabeth exclaimed in a loud voice, 'Blessed are you among women; and blessed is the child you will bear' (Luke 1:42), I can see Mary beaming with gratitude – to Elizabeth and to her God. It was a glorious confirmation for Mary that she had indeed found favor with God and that this was not all a dream or her imagination gone wild. Without a word from Mary, Elizabeth confirmed and blessed her. She rejoiced with Mary.

Have you ever thought about how different Elizabeth's reaction could have been? She was older than Mary, and a very godly woman. She had served God with her husband for years. She did not come from the infamous town of Nazareth. She had credentials and qualifications that outstripped Mary's. Why wasn't she chosen to bear the Son of God? Jealousy could have been her reaction. Envy could have consumed her. But instead she was able to 'rejoice with those who rejoice' (Rom. 12:15). Our human nature often finds it easier to 'mourn with those who mourn' than to rejoice with others, but Elizabeth didn't have that problem. She was thrilled for her cousin Mary, and gave her the warm welcome and loving confirmation Mary so needed at that time in her life.

Mary's Song

As we have already seen, we learn a great deal about Mary from her response to Elizabeth's greeting. Not only does it indicate a foundation of teaching and knowledge of Scripture, but it also shows us another reason Mary was highly favored: she focused on the blessing and had a praising heart.

Many women would have been focusing on the negatives of this situation. Many would have run to Elizabeth and said: 'Oh, Elizabeth, what am I going to do? What will I tell people? Will you shelter me? What will Joseph say? Help me, please, Elizabeth!' But Mary had an eternal point of view and a total trust in God, so that she was able to see the real importance of her position and was able to thank and praise God for His eternal purposes, though her life on earth was going to prove very difficult.

What a wonderful role model this simple lady is for us today. Do you have a heart of praise? That is what you need to find favor with God, as Mary did. How much time do you spend each day simply praising God for who He is and what He has done for you? Have you ever analyzed your prayer time? How much of it is just sheer praise to the Lord?

Notice that Mary used Scripture to recite back to the Lord in praise. That is a wonderful way to praise God. You could use her wonderful song for your own personal praise time.

A TIME APART

Mary spent three months with Elizabeth before returning to her home – three months in isolation, preparing herself for the very difficult road ahead. I would have loved to eavesdrop on the conversations between Mary and Elizabeth during that time. I have visited the town near Jerusalem where Elizabeth and Zechariah lived, and the town well where Elizabeth would have drawn her water is still there. As we stood by that well, I could hear echoes of the two of them, laughing, talking about their pregnancies, encouraging each other.

This was a first birth for both of them, and if you have been pregnant, you know how mysterious and frightening it can seem at times. These women did not have Dr. Spock's books to help, or LaMaze classes. Having babies back then was a very quiet affair; pregnant women were kept 'under cover' as much as possible. So, my guess is that the two of them were grateful for the time to talk between themselves about their upcoming motherhood.

What a joy for Elizabeth to have Mary there during her last trimester! Since Elizabeth was older, I am sure Mary's strong hands were welcome for many household chores and duties. But oh, what a blessing for Mary to have that three months with Elizabeth! I believe this godly woman mentored Mary during those months, passed on great scriptural knowledge to her, and taught her so much about God's laws and the promises concerning this Messiah-baby Mary was bearing.

Who knows just how important this three-month period was in the life of the most blessed woman who ever lived? Mary was a quiet woman who 'pondered things in her heart' often. I am certain there were many days later in her life when she pondered back to her time with Elizabeth, remembering her words of encouragement and her teaching, and finding great strength for the suffering and sorrow which were hers. Mary needed Elizabeth; Elizabeth needed Mary.

How wonderful it would be to see more of us spending time with godly women, learning from each other, growing with each other, whether in one-on-one friendships, small groups, or meetings. Mary and Elizabeth seemed to instinctively know they needed each other, and they took the time to be together. What wonderful fortification for the days ahead!

BACK HOME AGAIN

After those three months, Mary returned to Nazareth, and it is my opinion that this was when she broke the news to her family and to Joseph. She was ready for it then. We know how godly Joseph handled her announcement. Even before the angel of the Lord appeared to him in a dream, he was going to do for her the best he could – divorce her quietly in order to avoid public disgrace.

The custom of that day was that once a couple were engaged to be married, they were indeed bound as strongly as if their marriage vows had already been given. So, if someone wanted to get out of an engagement, there had to be a divorce. That was the option Joseph chose, because he knew it was the least painful for Mary. Under Jewish custom or law, it would not have been right for him to marry a pregnant woman. In fact, he could legally have had her stoned to death. I can imagine how he struggled with his decision. *I thought I knew Mary so well. Never in all my wildest imaginations would I have thought she would play around and get pregnant. How could this happen? Who is the father? Has Mary lost her mind?* I wonder how many sleepless nights Joseph spent after Mary broke the news to him!

I imagine Mary tried to tell him all about Gabriel and the miracle baby within her, but who could believe such a story? Would you have believed it? This had never happened before, nor would it ever happen again – a virgin birth! Do you think any of Mary's friends or even her family ever really believed that Jesus was born of a virgin? I wonder. My guess is that throughout her entire life very few people ever really believed she had conceived and given birth as a virgin. I believe she bore that disgrace as long as she lived.

But wonderful Joseph believed, once he was informed by the angel of the Lord of the true nature of Mary's pregnancy, and he became Mary's protector and provider. He took Mary home as his wife, but had no union with her until after she had given birth to Jesus. What a man! This cost him a great deal, I am sure. It sullied his reputation; people undoubtedly talked about him behind his back;

probably old friends dropped off; he may have lost respect in the town. Nevertheless, he stayed true to Mary, and what a great comfort he must have been to her throughout all their days together.

A VERY UNCOMFORTABLE JOURNEY

It is not necessary to retell the details of the birth of Jesus; I am sure you are familiar with the donkey ride to Bethlehem, the 'no rooms' condition in all the local inns, the inability of Joseph to find a proper place for Mary to deliver her baby.

I have always wondered if she delivered early, and if that is how they got caught in Bethlehem. Didn't they realize she was close to delivery when they left Nazareth? Indeed, women were not required to make this trip to register. It must have been a sudden decree that required Joseph to go at that time, and it could be that he did not want to leave Mary alone in Nazareth. She probably had few friends at that time who would help her with this birth; maybe even family members were reluctant to be a part of their lives because of the disgrace of her pregnancy. I believe Joseph made a conscious decision to take Mary with him in order to protect her, even though her due date was near.

AN UNUSUAL DELIVERY ROOM

If you knew, as Mary did, that you were bearing the Son of God, how would you feel when you realized that your delivery room was to be a smelly, damp stable? After all, Mary knew this child within her was of the Holy Spirit. Everyone else had to take it by faith, but Mary knew that she had never known a man, and yet here she was ready to give birth to a child. How could God allow His Son to be born in such a degrading manner? She must have been puzzled.

And then, almost adding insult to injury, while they were still in this terrible situation, just having given birth, in came these lowly shepherds to find this baby. We do not know how many there were, but they invaded Mary's delivery room. Not exactly what the reception committee would have planned for the King of kings and Lord of lords! But Mary allowed them in.

REARING A DIFFERENT CHILD

As Mary and Joseph brought Jesus up in that lowly town of Nazareth, there were many surprising and strange things that happened.

Rearing children is never easy. You learn early on that you have limited control over your child's behavior, attitudes, ambitions, friendships. It drives you to your knees probably more than any other role in life, as you recognize how helpless and inadequate you are for the task of teaching and training that human life entrusted to you.

The burden on Mary and Joseph must have been incredible as they watched Jesus grow. From the incident at the temple when he was twelve years old, we get a glimpse of the challenge they faced. Jesus was not a disobedient or rebellious child; in fact, He was a delight, but Mary and Joseph must have sensed right away that He marched to a different drummer and that someone else was in charge of His life.

MARY'S GROWN CHILD

We are given several jewels in Scripture that give us a glimpse into Mary's relationship with her divine Son once He left home and began His ministry.

The first is, of course, the famous first miracle when Jesus turned the water at a wedding into the best kind of wine, at his mother's request (John 2:1-11). What I love about this incident is the way Mary 'handled' Jesus. The people at the wedding were obviously good friends of hers, and running out of wine was a social disgrace. When she recognized the dilemma, she quietly said to her Son, 'They have no more wine.' Nothing else. No nagging, no demands, no suggestions. She just presented the problem to Him, knowing full well that He could do something about it. How did she know He could produce wine? Where did she think He was going to get more wine? Had He done something similar around the dinner table in her home previously, or was it simply that she had nowhere else to turn and just took a stab in the dark — maybe Jesus could find some more wine somewhere?

When she told Him the problem, He replied: 'Dear woman, why do you involve Me? My time has not yet come' (John 2:4). Jesus knew exactly what she wanted Him to do — to use His divine power and solve this problem for her friends. His first reaction is, 'Mom, not now. This is not the time for Me to reveal My power. I have other things to do first — more important than taking care of this small social dilemma of your good friends.'

Mary didn't argue with Him. She did not tell Him how to do it or when to do it; she did not threaten Him if He did not do it; she did not make any bargains with Him: 'I'll bake Your favorite pie tonight if You'll do this for me.' She did not try to manipulate Him: 'After all I've been through for You, couldn't You just do this one little thing for me? I don't ask much!' There was no female trickery on her part. She simply told the servants to do whatever Jesus told them to do, and went on her way, leaving the problem at His feet. Ah, no wonder this woman found favor with God! What a smart woman, and what quiet, strong faith she had.

In the scheme of His mission, providing wine for this poor, insignificant wedding was small potatoes for Jesus. Why would He bother? Especially since it might jeopardize God's timing for His ministry. You will remember how often during His ministry He instructed people not to reveal the miracle He had performed because He knew what a commotion it would cause. People always wanted something for nothing – free food, free health care, free wine! If word got out that all this was available from this nomadic preacher from Nazareth, it would make it difficult for Him to accomplish His primary mission and get His true message across.

Yet Mary never blinked an eye. This was important to her and her friends, no matter how small it was in world affairs, and she knew Jesus could solve the problem. So she did not hesitate to put it at His feet, with humility and acceptance, but also with expectation. And Jesus could not refuse her! He told the servants what to do and pretty soon they had the best wine ready to serve. I believe Mary's faith and her simple approach touched Jesus' heart and pleased Him. The fact that she was His mother also pulled on His heart strings, I am sure, but her quiet, strong faith in His ability to solve her small problem was more than He could resist.

We know that without faith it is impossible to please God. The reverse is also true. When the Lord sees our simple faith, it pleases Him and He is touched to work on our behalf, regardless of how small or insignificant our need may seem.

LETTING GO

My heart always goes out to Mary when I read about the time she and her other sons went to try to help Jesus. The story is found in Mark 3. Jesus was traveling all over, healing people and casting out demons. He was becoming very famous, so famous that He never had a moment to Himself and was mobbed everywhere He went.

Mark writes:'When His family heard about this, they went to take charge of Him, for they said, "He is out of His mind" (Mark 3:21). Jesus bewildered His family as much as everybody else – maybe more, because they knew Him as a brother, a son.

As they arrived at the house where Jesus was ministering, they could not even get in to see Him because of the mob. So they sent word inside that He should come out to see His mother and brothers. (There is no mention of Joseph here or at any other future point, which could indicate that he had died by this time and left Mary a widow.)

Jesus' response has often bothered me. It almost sounds cruel: 'Then He looked at those seated in a circle around Him and said, "Here are my mother and my brothers! Whoever does God's will is my brother and sister and mother"' (Mark 3:34–35). It almost seems like a slap in the face to His dear mother. What did He mean by this statement?

Well, knowing Jesus as we do, we can be certain He meant no disrespect to His mother. He treasured her greatly. On the cross, she was the one He thought of. He made certain of her welfare even as He hung there. He loved His mother.

But Jesus knew it was time to teach the world that He was not of this earth. He was not just that carpenter from Nazareth. He was on a divine mission from His Father, and everyone who chose to believe in Him could have a family relationship with Him. This request from His family gave Him an opportunity to make that point, and those listening would never forget His words. His heavenly calling took priority over His earthly family, important as that was.

I wonder if Mary heard His remark, if she knew what He had said? Probably not. They were separated by a mob. But she had to know that He no longer belonged to her. He was the Son of Man and the Son of God, and she had to let go of other motherly ties to this divine child of hers.

A PIERCING SWORD

Then the day came when Jesus had to go to the cross. Mary watched Him suffer and die. There she was, probably a widow, and her precious treasure, her miracle baby, was dying. Crucified, of all things.

As she stood at the cross, Mary must have remembered Simeon's prophetic words to her when they had presented the Baby Jesus at the temple for circumcision:

> This child is destined to cause the falling and rising of many in Israel, and to be a sign that will be spoken against, so that the thoughts of many hearts will be revealed. And a sword will pierce your own soul, too (Luke 2:34-35).

With a sword piercing her soul, Mary must have found it difficult to believe that she was 'blessed above all women.' Why was Jesus nailed to a cross like a criminal? It surely was no easier for her to accept and understand suffering than it is for us. She had done exactly what God had asked her to do; she had endured the disgrace, the exile in Egypt, the controversial reputation Jesus had. She had believed Gabriel and accepted her role in God's plan. How could it end in such disgrace?

It seems true that those who are used by God must inevitably go through this 'soul sword-piercing' in some form or another. If that is where you are now, be encouraged by this simple woman, Mary of Nazareth. It may be that you too have found favor with God, and He has a plan for you that necessitates suffering. Remember that God never takes us through times of suffering and sorrow capriciously, and He always goes with us every step of the way. His plan for us is always blessed, even when we can't see or feel it.

MARY'S GRACE-FULL LEGACY

As we have taken this closer look at Mary, the most blessed woman who ever lived, I hope you have seen that she was chosen for this honor in spite of her obvious inadequacies. She was a no-name woman from a disreputable town, without family connections, education or money. She was very shy and most likely very young, totally inexperienced, and lacking in eloquence, style or 'presence.' She would probably have been a disaster as a public speaker. She had never hobnobbed with the in-crowd. If it weren't for the infamy she must have had to endure because she had a baby out of wedlock, she would have gone unnoticed in most any group. You would not have been impressed with her credentials, gifts or her abilities.

Mary is the personification of 1 Corinthians 1:27-30:

But God chose the foolish things of the world to shame the wise; God chose the weak things of the world to shame the strong. He chose the lowly things of this world and the despised things – and the things that are not – to nullify the things that are, so that no one may boast before Him.

In our world of media-personality worshipers, we Christians tend to fall into that same trap of recognizing and honoring those who are in the public eye. Even in our evangelical circles, we put on pedestals those who are dynamic speakers, outstanding musicians, or performers in some other noticeable way. This instills into our thinking the false notion that these people are more qualified and more usable in God's service.

That is not true, and we need to continually remind ourselves of the truth of this passage from 1 Corinthians. Mary was a foolish, weak and despised person, used by God in a great way. She did not deserve it; she did not earn it; she did not qualify. God looked down and found a woman who met His qualifications – foolish, weak and despised – and made a showpiece of her. That is what grace is all about.

Have you been comparing yourself to others and feeling that you do not have the necessary qualifications to be of real worth to Jesus? Well, you should have just the opposite reaction. Recognizing your total inadequacy places you in good company with Mary, the mother of Jesus, and makes you a candidate for a profound display of God's grace. You see, when God reaches down to you and makes something beautiful out of your life, as only He can do, you will never try to take credit for it. You will give Him all the glory. That is why God looks for the weak and foolish things to use.

I look forward to a leisurely conversation in heaven with Mary someday, when I can ask her all the questions I have about her life as Jesus' mother. I am quite certain that she will share the joy and blessing that was hers, but she will insist that it was all a demonstration of God's astonishing grace to a simple, trusting and totally unworthy woman.

Nancy seemed to have just an ordinary life. She married young, had children, and served in the church joyfully with her husband. Then, like Mary, one day her whole world changed.

11

Nancy's Story

Nancy has never had a halo either, but like Mary of Nazareth, she wants to please God and be the godly woman He wants her to be. She wants to find favor with God, as Mary of Nazareth did.

Nancy is petite, sophisticated, mature, warm and loving, the kind of person who makes lots of friends. Despite her charm, her story is one of deception and a loss of innocence like few I have ever heard.

A Naive Beginning

Nancy was married after her freshman year of college. She had met the ideal man who looked and seemed as though he was made for her. Together they were a 'cute' couple, the kind that would catch your attention when they walked into a room, and they had personalities to match. Don was charming, good looking, talented and ambitious. Nancy felt she had made a wise choice, and she was delighted to be his wife.

Their first child, a daughter, Susan, was born after Nancy's sophomore year in college. She was thrilled to be a mom. After they both had graduated from their Midwest college, they moved to Cleveland, Ohio, where Don entered medical school. They applied to various country clubs as lifeguards, trying to earn some extra money for Don's medical school. At the Lakeshore Club they met a couple who had four girls and a baby boy. This couple had recently found new life in Christ, and they invited Nancy and Don to come to their Baptist church. Nancy and Don were faithful churchgoers and thought they were adequately religious, so at first they refused the invitation, but the love and warmth of this couple eventually convinced them to visit. At the church they heard the Gospel clearly presented, and they both made a genuine commitment to Christ. Their little family now became a Christian family.

Nancy embraced her new life in Christ with all her heart, and she determined to be the best wife and mother she could possibly be. That was, after all, her calling from God, and she truly wanted to please God. Don was very gifted musically, and he became active in the church's music program, directing the choir, playing the organ and singing.

However, Don decided to abandon his medical education, and he began trying to find the right job.

EARLY HEARTACHES

Four years after Susan was born, Nancy had another child, who was born with a heart defect. The baby eventually died. Nancy was only 24 years old and a very new Christian at the time. While the death of this baby was painful, in childlike faith she placed her trust in the Lord and waited expectantly for Him to give her another baby.

Four years later, after going through the ordeal that a barren woman goes through – praying, temperature taking, counting days – the couple finally had a healthy baby boy. Nancy and Don were ecstatic. Nancy had prayed Hannah's prayer for a son, and she gladly dedicated her baby to the Lord, as Hannah had done. Her faith was strengthened and she became even more committed to following Jesus.

A SHELTERED ENVIRONMENT

The church Nancy and Don attended held some very strict rules of behavior for their members. She was expected to wear no makeup, never cut her hair, never go to movies, smoke, drink or play cards. None of that was a problem to her because she was eager to please God; Nancy went along with it all.

Living in this very sheltered community, Nancy was taught her role as a mother and wife, and she enthusiastically threw herself into it. She loved baking, sewing, cleaning and taking care of her babies. She was blissful in her safe world and continued to grow in her knowledge of God's Word.

Don never seemed to be able to settle into the right job and, with his many job changes, their finances were often difficult. Even that did not daunt Nancy's joy, as she just tried to make their money go further by being a better wife and mother.

A year and a half after her son's birth, Abigail was born, and two years later Anne. With three girls and one son, Nancy felt she had the perfect home. She felt fulfilled in her role and was content with her life.

THE YEARS GO BY

As the children grew, her involvement in church and Bible studies grew as well. She and Don taught Sunday school, and together they taught a couple's Bible study. As their children became involved in the church's youth groups, they became leaders there also. As Nancy puts it: 'We were just buzzing along in our happy Christian life.'

The only fly in their ointment, from Nancy's perspective, was Don's roller-coaster career. He could never seem to find the right fit, and he moved from one job to another, always assuring Nancy that 'the right deal' was just around the next corner. Nancy saw her role as being supportive of his dreams, and she always tried to encourage him. She learned how to survive through the feast and famine scenarios.

When their oldest daughter, Susan, was a senior in high school, Don became very sick with hepatitis for almost a year. That was a difficult time for the family in many ways, but Nancy has a very optimistic nature, and she had learned to trust the Lord. She would sit and read Christian biographies to Don while he was sick, and elders from their church would come regularly to visit and encourage them.

The family chose Wheaton College (Illinois) for Susan after high school, and that was another dream come true for Nancy. Even with the temporary setback from Don's illness, she felt God had His hand on her family and that they were in His care.

GROWING STRESS

As Susan went away to college, Don suggested they move to the East Coast where he would have better business opportunities. He insisted this would be the best thing for the family financially, and

Nancy saw it as her duty to be obedient to her husband's leadership. So they prepared to move.

This was not an easy thing for Nancy. To bolster her faith, she took hymn books and went through them page by page, singing them and saying, 'This applies to us moving to Atlantic City, New Jersey.' She wanted so much to know that this was God's plan for their family. There were nagging worries in the back of her mind about this move, but she was convinced that her duty was to take care of the home and family, trusting her husband to make the right financial and business decisions. She thought what she was doing was right because she was submissive to Don and supportive of him. Wasn't that what God required of a good wife?

THE DARK DAYS BEGIN

The wonderful job in Atlantic City did not work out the way Don had planned, so he started traveling back and forth to New York City on a regular basis, working on putting together some 'big deals' involving commodities and other things that were over Nancy's head. She could not understand what he was doing. There were weird phone calls in the middle of the night and sudden trips; but again, she trusted God and her husband to do the right thing for her family.

Naturally, they looked for and found a good church home in New Jersey, and they again got involved. Don was active in the music, and Nancy found a home Bible study for herself. She felt this was confirmation that this was God's plan for their lives.

The finances, however, kept getting worse and worse. When the bills could not be paid, Nancy had to endure the embarrassment of cars being taken away and sheriffs knocking on her door to say they were behind in their rent or other payments. This confused Nancy greatly, but Don always seemed to have answers, and he kept assuring her that the 'deal' he needed was right around the corner and things would be better soon.

LIFE UNRAVELS

With Don away in New York more and more, and the bills piling higher and higher, Nancy decided she should earn some money. She went to work for Prudential Bache as a secretary. All the time, her husband was working on real estate deals that never materialized, and Nancy's modest salary was the only steady income they had.

Coming home from work one day, Don and Nancy noticed their son Nathan and his girlfriend sitting on the front step of their rented house on the beach. There was a sign on the door from the sheriff refusing to give them entry into their home. Her son asked; 'What does this mean?' Nancy knew what it meant. They had not paid their rent for six months, and the landlord had finally taken legal action against them.

Three weeks later, the landlord moved everything out of the house and took all their furniture except Don's piano and the refrigerator, which were too heavy to move. He seized all their property to pay for the back rent. They were allowed to go in and remove their clothes and personal items, but everything else was gone.

The shame and embarrassment were almost more than Nancy could handle. The children lied to their friends in order to cover up, explaining that they were looking for a better house to rent. Meanwhile, some dear friends at their church let Nancy and the kids live with them for a while.

You may wonder how it ever got to this point before Nancy started to question her husband and his many deals. 'I don't know why I wasn't asking more questions,' Nancy says today. 'I believed in my husband; I really did think some deal was going to come through. I felt I was in submission and obedience, and I was trying to do the very best I could with what I thought my responsibility was.'

A SPLIT FAMILY

Nancy's husband was spending more and more time in New York, and Nancy was thinking of taking her teenagers and moving back home with her family in Indiana. Her friends encouraged Don to stay in New York for a while and work on the financial situation. So, on January 1, 1982, he moved to New York, and they lived apart.

Every day after work Nancy would walk home from the bus stop eight blocks away, crying all the way. Life was miserable; all her dreams were dashed. She could not figure out what had happened to her blissful Christian family.

The kids quit after-school activities so they could work. They all saved their money carefully for six months so they could move into their own apartment. She had everything budgeted out exactly to the penny, in order to get by on her income and the money the children earned.

Don was sick a great deal, in and out of hospitals, but Nancy never knew exactly what was wrong with him. He was staying with a man in New York named Greg, who was active in a church in the Village. Nancy met him and talked with him a couple of times. He told her that Don was having chemo treatments, but he would say nothing more. 'He must have cancer,' Nancy said, but no answers were forthcoming.

When Don was in the hospital, she called and spoke to the doctor, who told her, 'If your husband wants to tell you about his condition, he can. But I think he should tell you.' The only thing she could figure out was that Don must have cancer and not want her to know.

Nancy stopped teaching Bible studies and certainly did not have the same fellowship with the Lord she had had before, but the children were still going to church and youth groups and they still kept up appearances as much as possible. With the shame of being thrown out of her home, she found it difficult to go back to her church and face her friends. After all, Don had been the music director at that church, and she was very embarrassed by his failure and his disappearance, leaving the family as he did.

DEATH STRIKES TWICE

Don stayed in New York, getting sicker and not being able to work. Nancy went to New York to see him a couple of times. It was very strained and very stressful to be with him. He looked worse and worse, lost his hair, and was obviously not doing well physically, but still there was no explanation. She continued to think he must have cancer.

A whole year went by, and Nancy began studying to become a stockbroker. In February of 1983 she and Abigail went to New York, where Nancy had arranged to take her stockbroker's exam, and they went to see Don, who was again in the hospital.

When they arrived in New York, Nancy called the hospital to find out what was wrong with Don, but she never got any answers. He was in Bellevue, which is New York's charity hospital, and when she and Abigail went in to talk to Don's doctor, they were finally told the bad news: 'Your husband has AIDS.' AIDS? Nancy recalled reading something about this in the *New York Times*. Abigail recalled an article in *People* magazine. Between the two of them, they pieced the truth together: AIDS was an incurable disease primarily caused through homosexual relationships. For the first time, Nancy knew the truth about Don. Until that moment, she never had suspected it. 'There were two things so far from my mind that I truly never considered them: divorce and homosexuality,' Nancy says. When she saw him that weekend he was incoherent, and Nancy never had another rational conversation with him.

Nathan drove up with some friends the next day, and he saw his father one last time. They returned home, and Nancy broke the news to Anne on their return, and at thirteen years of age, her response was astounding to Nancy: 'I'm not surprised,' she said.

Finally, they all knew the truth that had evaded them through the years. Two weeks later Don died. Nancy never had a conversation with him about his illness or the other life he had been living throughout most of their marriage. He never admitted his sin, never apologized, never explained. There are questions for Nancy that will go unanswered until eternity.

Nancy and her children had to face the death of their husband and father, as well as the implications of his illness. It was overwhelming, to say the least. Nancy eventually learned that Don had been diagnosed with AIDS over a year before he died, but she never knew, until two weeks before his death.

Painful as all this was, Don's death brought some relief for Nancy and the children. No longer did they have to wonder what he was doing, when he was going to make a living. No longer was she confused about events in his life that had puzzled her so often in the past: the late nights coming home, the lack of support, the mysterious trips to New York, the unexplained meetings in the middle of the night, his inability to get his act together and get a job, the undiagnosed illnesses.

Nancy's lack of knowledge about AIDS and the slow process of getting appropriate information was a major problem. She did not know enough – and no one told her – to be tested herself for the HIV virus; it was years before she knew to do that. There was no counseling for the family to help them understand this horrible situation. No one talked about it; there was a great deal of denial. They all toughed it out on their own.

When Don died, the church seemed not to know what to do, and so they did nothing. True, Nancy had stopped attending by that time, but Don had been the choir director, and Nathan and Anne still attended. There was no safety net for Nancy and the children.

Nancy felt both anger and shame. She began to go through a deep spiritual depression, struggling with the aftermath of learning that she had been married to a bisexual man and the loss of self-image that has to accompany such a revelation. She desperately needed someone to love her, hold her and give her back her sense of wholeness. She began to meet men, and tried to find some happiness in relationships. It doesn't take a psychologist to see how a woman in her position would be shattered in this situation and feel an overwhelming need to be loved in the right way by a 'normal' man. So, in this way, Nancy tried to find some relief from the constant pain.

Three months after Don's death, as they were all trying to find some firm footing for their lives, Nancy went through every mother's worst nightmare – the death of a child. She had gone to New York for a weekend visit with a friend. On Saturday morning she called another friend just to talk, and he said, 'Nancy, we've been trying to reach you. You need to call the New Jersey State Police.' Refusing to give her any further information, she called the police. 'Your son has been involved in an accident,' came the stock answer when Nancy called. With further probing she was told that he had indeed been killed in the accident.

In a state of total shock, Nancy called her married daughter, Susan, who had moved to Chicago with her husband. She can still hear the screams that came from the telephone as she gave Susan this horrific news.

Her friend drove her back to New Jersey in an old convertible. It was a cool day, but they put the top down. She wore his leather jacket, and for two and a half hours they rode in morbid silence. What was there to say? This latest blow was more than Nancy's mind could comprehend. Only one week from his high school graduation, Nathan's accident seemed like a slap in her face, a swift kick while she was down. How much more could she take?

Nathan was her gift from God that she had dedicated back to the Lord. Why would God take Nathan away when she needed him most? 'This is not the God I know,' she said. 'I know a loving God;

this is not the God I know.' While she never raised her fist to God, she quit calling Him holy, because she thought that would mean she agreed with what He did, and she certainly did not agree with what He had done. She found she could no longer worship God because of all the terrible things that had happened to her.

The church that Nancy and Don had attended was wonderful in Nathan's death. They now had somewhere to put their grief, and they poured out love and help to Nancy and the girls. Nancy had been unable to make any plans, and when Susan arrived from Chicago, she took over the necessary details for Nathan's funeral. Nancy could hardly lift her head off her pillow, and she spent those days in deep pain.

When they drove to the church for Nathan's memorial service, Nancy was amazed to see that there were lines of people waiting to get in. It looked like the entire high school student body was there; all of Nancy's co-workers came, and all of her church family. This outpouring of support touched Nancy deeply and still gives her comfort as she recalls Nathan's funeral.

RUNNING AWAY

After Nathan was killed, someone said, 'You need to leave the East Coast; you've paid your dues to the East Coast.' So, Nancy moved to Chicago to be near her married daughter, Susan, and her grandchildren. Abigail was now attending Wheaton College as well, so it seemed the logical move to make. She was able to transfer with her company to the Chicago office.

Don died in March of 1983, Nathan was killed in June, and Nancy moved to Chicago in August. But moving away did not dull the pain inside. Confusion, anger and bewilderment combined with her great need and vulnerability at the time, and Nancy found that her lifestyle continued to slide once she moved to Chicago.

'I wanted to get out of the relationships that I was bound in, but I was truly bound,' Nancy says. 'I would come out of church on Sunday, and I would cry and I would want to leave those relationships. But I could not. I did not know what I would do if I did not have that emotional support from this person or that person. And that was bondage. I realized that I was in bondage, but I couldn't get free.'

That went on for six years. Nancy wanted to be close again with God, but she wasn't sure she ever would be. Yet there was still that longing in her heart to be like Jesus and to please Him.

It was during her first months in Chicago that I met Nancy, through mutual friends. The pain in her eyes was unmistakable, and her heartache was palpable. I knew she needed help, and I knew she was looking for it in the wrong places, as I had done in my own life. We had some heart-wrenching conversations, but Nancy wasn't yet at a place where she could turn back to the God who seemingly had betrayed her. Our paths parted during her six years in that spiritual desert, but they were to come back together again in a beautiful way.

A GRATEFUL HEART

Sensing a great need to be back in fellowship with God, Nancy decided to go by herself to a Christian seminar being held in Chicago. As she got there, she prayed that somebody she knew from her church would be there. A wonderful woman from church walked in and sat with her, and Nancy knew this was a part of God's plan.

The speaker said: 'You have to have a grateful heart.' That was the one thing Nancy just could not do. She did not have a grateful heart. How could she be grateful for a deceptive marriage and the death of her son?

As Nancy got in the car with Judy that night, she said, 'I can't have a grateful heart, but I want to. I know that is what it is going to take to get me out of bondage.' She went home that night and looked at Nathan's picture on the table by her bed. Slowly, deliberately, she took his picture in her arms and knelt down beside her bed. Hesitatingly, slowly, she started thanking God that she had had him for eighteen years. She started being thankful for all the wonderful things about Nathan. He was a great kid. All the kids loved him, and he loved everybody. She found she could be sincerely grateful for the years she had had Nathan.

Then she thought, 'I guess I have to thank God for my husband too. I guess I have to thank God that I have my children from my marriage to Don in order to have a grateful heart.' To be grateful for that was much more difficult, and she was a long time on her knees with a battle going on inside of her. But finally, that night, God gave her the grace to be grateful even for Don, and for the first time in many years she had a sense of the presence of God once again.

A RENEWED LIFE

Nancy knew she had to begin to make right choices in her life. She had to abandon the illicit relationships that she had looked to for support and strength. Though they had never met her need, it was fearful to think of giving them up, but she began hanging up the phone when certain men called. She stopped going to meetings where she knew she would have to encounter these men. She began the hard work of renewing her relationship with the Lord.

Since she had not read her Bible for six years, she had to start that discipline anew in her life. For two years she could not read anything but the Psalms. She had been broken, and in this healing process, the Psalms touched her deeply. She went to church, and the music became a healing force for her. Then she learned to pray again. 'All those disciplines were gone out of my life,' Nancy says, 'but I wanted to be back with God; I wanted to walk with Him again.'

AN OUTREACH TO OTHERS

Nancy has learned how to deal gently with others because of the great pain in her own life. Now, when she sees a Christian woman who is getting her needs met in the wrong way, it does not surprise her. She has had her eyes opened to another world, and her heart really has been softened. She has compassion for her children and the people in her life as never before, and God now brings many women into her life for her special touch.

She encouraged me to teach a class with her for women at our church, which we began in 1993. I saw the compassion and tenderness she had for these dear sisters in Christ and how beautifully she related to their pain and struggle. It has been such a thrill to be a witness to God's transforming power in Nancy.

She has gone on to earn a degree in counseling, and now uses her education and life experiences to help others with their struggles.

THE ABUNDANT-LIFE TRACK

Nancy's own words best express what her life is like now: 'If there were a great Christian man, I'd love to be married again, but I know I can take my needs to Jesus. If I have a yearning, I know that will pass. I go to Him and tell Him, and I know it will pass. I do not get my needs met in an illegitimate way anymore. I am back in the abundant-life track now.'

Life has brought more hardship for Nancy. Her oldest daughter, Susan, fought a battle with brain cancer for many years, and after going into submission, it resurfaced recently, and now Susan has passed on. So Nancy is left with her two daughters, Abigail and Anne, and Anne has distanced herself from her family and seems to be fighting her own inner battles. Yet Nancy knows that her only source of strength is Jesus Christ, and she finds her needs met in Him.

Nancy is again finding favor with God, as Mary of Nazareth did, and the joy of her salvation has been restored. She reeks with thankfulness and victory when you are with her, and the grace of God is evident in her face. She has known what it is to be at the bottom, and she knows the reality of this astonishing grace of God. It has set her free.

12

THE SAMARITAN WOMAN'S STORY

This woman we have called 'the Woman at the Well' had to live with the consequences of her past, and that meant years of isolation and rejection.

John recorded her encounter with Jesus at Jacob's well in Sychar, Samaria, in the fourth chapter of his gospel (John 4:1–42). For many reasons, it is one of my favorite passages in all of the gospels, but mostly because of the way Jesus interacted with this woman of disrepute. By this point in her life, she must have felt there was no hope for her. She was a survivor, but one whose daily life was dreary drudgery.

HER BACKGROUND

Undoubtedly this Samaritan woman was poor. Women of affluence did not draw water; they had servants to do that for them. And it was not usual to draw water in the middle of a hot Samaritan day. The well – Jacob's well – was a half-mile or more out of town. Most women would have used the town well in the cool part of the day. Maybe this Samaritan woman purposefully chose this time to draw water in order to avoid the other women. Given her current situation, the other women may have wanted nothing to do with her.

We know that she had been married five times and was now living with a sixth man. We do not know why she had gone through so many marriages, but it is doubtful that she was widowed five times. The fact that she was now living with a man might indicate that she had given up and settled for anyone available. It certainly shows a decline in her morals.

It is also likely that she had been abandoned by the men she had married, since women rarely, if ever, did the divorcing. The law allowed men great latitude in disposing of an unsatisfactory wife. The chief excuse for divorce was barrenness. If a woman could not bear a son, that was grounds for divorce. Could it have been that this lonely woman had not only been abandoned and divorced by five men, but also had suffered the pain of barrenness?

HER ENCOUNTER WITH JESUS

The fact that she even had an encounter with Jesus is amazing, for three reasons:

- In that culture men never spoke to women in public, not even their wives, mothers or sisters.
- Jewish men never spoke to Samaritans. Samaritans were 'half-breeds,' Jews who had intermarried with foreigners and were considered outcasts by 'true' Jews. They hated each other; a Jew would avoid even going through Samaria.
- No self-respecting man, especially a teacher, would ever speak to a woman of such ill repute as was this Samaritan woman.

So, you can imagine her surprise when Jesus began the conversation by asking her, 'Will you give me a drink?' (John 4:7). He took the initiative and ignored tradition to bridge the gap. Yes, she was surprised, but she was also suspicious.

Her response was less than courteous: 'You are a Jew and I am a Samaritan woman. How can you ask me for a drink?' (John 4:9). I can understand how she felt. Men had always taken advantage of her; she probably didn't trust any of them any longer, and here was another one asking another favor! She must have thought that He wanted more than a drink of water from her, and that this was simply His way of 'hitting on her.' She also got in her digs about the racial prejudice of the Jews, as she sarcastically reminded Him that He was not supposed to even speak to her.

One of the things I love best about Jesus is His gentle nature. Notice how gently He replied in verse 10: 'If you knew the gift of

God and who it is that asks you for a drink, you would have asked Him and He would have given you living water.' His reply to this woman's ungracious manner was gentle – strength under control. That is because He could see beyond the tough exterior to her broken heart.

You know, usually when someone is hard on the outside, it is a covering for the pain that is underneath. If we could just learn to look beyond people's harsh words or rude manner and see their hearts, as Jesus did with this woman, we would be more able to reach them with His love.

HER CHANGED ATTITUDE

Proverbs 15:1 says, 'A gentle answer turns away wrath, but a harsh word stirs up anger.' Jesus' gentle answer seemed to change her attitude toward Him. It also made her curious to find out about this special water. She referred to him next as 'Sir.' I'm certain His voice and manner were so different that she could not continue to be defensive. His approach to her was kind and conciliatory, and she could not resist. She proceeded to ask a practical question:

> Sir, you have nothing to draw with and the well is deep. Where can you get this living water? Are you greater than our father Jacob, who gave us the well and drank from it himself, as did also his sons and his flocks and herds? (John 4:11–12)

This Man promised her something wonderful and special, something she had never had before – living water. Yet she responded with questions and doubts.

How many times have I done the same thing? This Samaritan woman had an excuse. She didn't know who she was talking to at this point. Sometimes I act as if I do not know who I am talking to either. I either do not understand or I forget God's power, His majesty, His love, His care, His nature, His character. I want to see, not trust. I forget that God rarely works the way I do, and that He does not need buckets to draw water. Indeed, He can 'do immeasurably more than all we ask or imagine, according to His power that is at work within us' (Eph. 3:20).

JESUS' INCREDIBLE OFFER

To her question of doubt, Jesus could have replied very abruptly: 'Wait a minute, lady, you don't know who you're talking to. I'm Jesus of Nazareth. I'm the One who has been performing miracles all over the place. How dare you question My word!' He could have told her all the things He had done, informed her of His miracles, His reputation, His power. Instead, He told her all the things she had done and offered her eternal water!

You see, Jesus' request for water was not because He was thirsty. It was His way of opening up a conversation so that He could give this woman what she so desperately needed – a spring of water inside of her welling up to eternal life. Therefore, when she showed doubts about His claim to provide living water, He used that as an opportunity to impart truth to her. He had no need to defend Himself; this conversation was for her benefit. What a great model for personal witnessing we have in this story. Jesus was the original 'lifestyle witnesser.'

Notice that Jesus asked her for a drink of water, and then He offered her a well of water. It is always that way with Jesus. He asks us to give Him our meager hearts and wills, and then He gives us abundant life in return. Isaiah 61:3 puts it so beautifully: '...to bestow on them a crown of beauty instead of ashes, the oil of gladness instead of mourning, and a garment of praise instead of a spirit of despair.' That is the exchange rate we get with Jesus, and it is another example of His astonishing grace. Something for nothing. Everything for nothing. Marvelous grace.

This Samaritan woman knew a good deal when she heard it, and she said, 'Sir, give me this water so that I won't get thirsty and have to keep coming here to draw water' (John 4:15). You see, she was still thinking on the human level. Drawing water every day, in the heat, was not her favorite duty. If she could find some way to avoid this back-breaking job, that would be wonderful for her. Her initial attraction to Jesus was a selfish one; He seemed to offer her a way out of this drudgery.

Do not be too hard on her. We have all done it! We are by nature selfish creatures, and our natural reaction is to get whatever we can for ourselves. So, even in our relationship with Jesus, we are often in it for what He offers. That is certainly the way our relationship with Jesus begins. We come because He offers eternal life. But a growing

Christian should soon see beyond the gift to the Giver. A verse from an A. B. Simpson hymn, 'Himself,' puts it so well:

Once it was the blessing,
Now it is the Lord,
Once it was the feeding,
Now it is His Word;
Once His gifts I wanted,
Now the Giver own;
Once I sought for healing,
Now for Him alone.

AN UNUSUAL APPROACH

Jesus' next statement to this woman was startling. As He so often did, He completely changed the subject, seemingly ignored her request for water, shifted gears, and said, 'Go, call your husband and come back' (John 4:16). What does a husband have to do with living water?

Jesus knew, of course, that she had no husband; He knew her reputation. But He also knew that she had to see her own need, her own condition, before she was a candidate for His living water. She had to humbly confess the current mess of her life. Regardless of who had mistreated her or how she had ended up where she was, she could no longer shift the blame and offer excuses. She had to take responsibility for her sin.

It is no different when we come to Jesus. We must understand who we are and know that He knows all about us, realizing that it is useless to try to hide anything from Him. We have to abandon our excuses, our blame-shifting, and accept responsibility for the sinful condition of our lives.

To this woman he said, 'Go, call your husband,' in order to get to the sin problem in her life. What would He say to you or me?

He asked this question of 'the Woman at the Well' not to embarrass her or shame her, but to help her. Jesus never condemns us, but He does confront us with the sinful areas of our lives that are keeping us from His living water. In order to find spiritual healing, we must expose the cancerous sin in our lives. However, the good news is that we cannot tell Jesus anything He does not already know about us. He knows the worst yet still wants to give us His living water.

In his book *Knowing God*, J. I. Packer puts this so well:

> There is tremendous relief in knowing that His love to me is utterly realistic, based at every point on prior knowledge of the worst about me, so that no discovery now can disillusion Him about me, in the way I am so often disillusioned about myself, and quench His determination to bless me ... for some unfathomable reason, He wants me as His friend, and desires to be my friend.[1]

Jesus did not need to be told about the Samaritan woman's past life, but she needed to confess it. He dealt privately with her. He dealt without condemnation or severity, and He was gentle and kind, but He dealt with her sin because that was her basic problem. Jesus meets us where we are in our sin, but He will always confront it.

At this point in their conversation, Jesus astonished her by revealing His knowledge of her five marriages. She realized that He was no ordinary man, and acknowledged that He must be a prophet. So, she steered the conversation toward a controversial topic of the day: where was the proper place to worship? 'Our fathers worshiped on this mountain, but you Jews claim that the place where we must worship is Jerusalem' (John 4:20).

I think she was uncomfortable with the direction the conversation was taking. Jesus was too close for comfort – too close to her heart, too close to her pain, too close to her need. The Lord had gently fingered her and she was embarrassed. So, she put on her religious face and started the 'what church do you go to?' conversation. Aren't we all a bit uncomfortable when we have to face ourselves?

AN ASTONISHING REVELATION

Jesus responded by giving her the truth about worship. He set her straight theologically: 'You Samaritans worship what you do not know; we worship what we do know, for salvation is from the Jews' (John 4:22). Correct theology is important. Jesus could not allow her faulty understanding about worship to go unchallenged, because only truth will set people free. Jesus was gentle with her, but He was not intimidated in any way. He told her the truth.

Next, Jesus revealed a profound insight into worship and worshipers. Untold numbers of sermons have been preached on

1. J. I. Packer, *Knowing God*, Downers Grove, Ill.: InterVarsity Press, 1973, p. 37.

these four verses (John 4:21-24). We learn that worship has two elements: spirit and truth. We must worship with our hearts and our emotions, but worship must also be based on biblical truth. Our spirit communicates with His Spirit when we worship truly. One of the most important things we learn here is that God the Father seeks worshipers. Worship must be a cornerstone of our daily lives in order for us to please God.

I think 'the Woman at the Well' struggled with how to handle this unusual conversation with this unique man. She scrambled to make sense of it all, so she replied: 'I know that Messiah (called Christ) is coming. When He comes, He will explain everything to us' (John 4:25). It was her way of saying, 'Well, we can't understand all of this but when the Messiah comes, He'll explain it all.' I believe it was her attempt to stop this conversation about God and worship because she was in over her head and she knew it.

I have often seen people do the same thing. As soon as the truth of the Gospel starts getting close to their heart, they will say, 'Well, it's all a matter of how you interpret the Bible, and nobody really knows the whole truth;' or, 'I guess it's just a difference in the way people interpret the Bible.' But the facts are that the Messiah has spoken, and we can assertively proclaim His truth.

Jesus certainly did so with the Samaritan woman: 'I who speak to you am He' (John 4:26). Whoa! His words could not have been clearer. They must have rocked her back on her heels! This Man just claimed to be the Messiah. Was it true? How could it be true? Should she believe Him? Her mind must have been spinning at this point.

But what astonishes me most is that Jesus chose this time and this woman to reveal these great truths. It was the first time in His ministry that Jesus openly said in unequivocal words that He was the Messiah. Wouldn't you think He would have chosen a public occasion to say this? Why did He do so now, with this woman of disrepute?

Because she needed to know to whom she was talking, so that she could make a decision about this living water. She needed to be confronted with the claims of the Messiah on her life. He was not going to allow her to go back to town without making a decision. Either she believed He was the Messiah or she did not.

GRACE FOR THE SAMARITAN WOMAN

Their conversation was interrupted at this time by the return of the disciples, who were astonished to find Jesus talking with this woman. They immediately recognized how unworthy she was to have a conversation with the Master. None of them would have engaged her in a conversation! Even without knowing the details of her past, the disciples were undoubtedly prejudiced against Samaritans and against women, as were most Jewish men of that day. Jesus gave them a great example of how He breaks down walls of prejudice and bigotry.

Certainly the Samaritan woman did not miss the significance of her conversation with this unusual Man. She knew her lowly state; she knew her many failures; she knew her sinful lifestyle. Yet Jesus had openly and gently reached out to her, ignoring the cultural barriers and social bias of the day.

I am sure she did not want to stay around once these twelve men arrived, so she hurried back to the town, leaving her water jar behind in her haste. She seemed to forget her inhibitions at this point. She simply rushed back to town saying, 'Come, see a man who told me everything I ever did. Could this be the Christ?' (John 4:29).

Because of her urging and her testimony, many made their way to the well to find out who this Person was who had impressed this Samaritan woman so greatly. And because of her testimony, because she led them to Jesus, many Samaritans believed in Him. At their urging, Jesus stayed two more days in Samaria, where He taught all who wanted to listen. 'And because of His words many more became believers' (John 4:41).

I think it is interesting that John tells us she left her water jar behind when she rushed back into town. What a small detail to include in this story. Think of what that water jar represented: her daily burden. She had to carry it back and forth every day, and from her prior reaction, we know she wanted to be rid of that humiliating, tiring, boring, never-ending burden in her life. That water jar was evidence of her poverty and her low estate in life.

We aren't given any more details about the life of this Samaritan woman, but I am convinced she was a changed woman after her encounter with Jesus. I believe she chose to live a pure life after this. I look forward to meeting her in heaven and hearing the rest of her story.

The grace of God reached down to a poor, outcast woman on a hot day in Samaria, and with incredible gentleness, that grace touched her, taught her and changed her forever. That is the way it is with the grace of our Lord Jesus Christ.

GRACE FOR US

Have you left your water jar at Jesus' feet? That water jar is the symbol of the burdens and sins we carry around until we meet the Savior. Then, when we discover He wants to give us living water, we realize there is no more need for the water jar. We can be rid of that burden. We can put that water jar right at the feet of Jesus and go out to tell others about Him, free from our burden, free from our guilt, free from the humiliation of our past, free from who we are!

Do you know freedom from your sins and your past? You can do so right now by confessing your sins and accepting Him as your Messiah.

Maybe you have done that, but you sometimes go back and get that old water jar. Have you been trying to carry your own burdens lately? Perhaps you keep living under the heavy load of past sins and guilt. Jesus is waiting at the well of eternal water, and you can leave that water jar right at His feet and go forward again, with freedom.

In the next chapter you will read the story of Camille. Like the Samaritan woman, she had a string of men in her life. With those relationships came abuse, depression, and heartbreak. Then Camille came to the 'well.'

13

CAMILLE'S STORY

Camille almost ruined her life because of her desire for men. A life-long search for a man to take her father's place led her to do some very foolish things. If you met Camille today, you would never guess the past history – the baggage – that is behind her classical good looks and vivacious smile. You would be impressed with her intellect, her articulateness, her confident manner and her warmth, but she has not arrived at this point in her life's journey without a great deal of pain and struggle.

Her story follows, mostly in her own words – and if you think it could not have happened to one person in one lifetime, let me assure you it did, and she is still in the prime of life. It is a wonderful story of God's grace.

AN IDYLLIC CHILDHOOD

Born as an only child into a privileged Southern family, Camille was loved, pampered, protected and adored by her father. Her mother reared her by strict Christian principles, as was customary in many Southern families, going to church three times each week and twice on Sundays. Camille knew every Bible story by heart, and church was an integral part of her life. She loved to line up her dolls on the living room sofa and preach to them God's plan of salvation.

Growing up alone in the country on a cattle ranch was a solitary but idyllic childhood. She roamed the pastures, climbed trees, rode her horse, and developed a great love for books at an early age.

THE SHATTERED DREAM

Her idyllic childhood came to an abrupt end at the age of nine when her father died suddenly. After being in the hospital for over two weeks, her father was brought home early on a Sunday morning, with every hope of total rehabilitation from his coronary attack. Camille wanted to stay with him that Sunday morning, but her mother and aunts told her it would be best for her to go to church with her cousins.

During the service they brought word to her aunt that her father had died. She recalls the deadly silence of that Sunday morning and the ride home that she thought would never end. Her profound disappointment in being denied those final hours with her father intensified her grief and confusion.

As was the custom in that Southern town, her father's body was laid out at their home. Her family urged her to view the body of her father, but she refused. She wanted to remember him as he was, and she was not yet prepared to accept his death.

For months she lived in complete denial and would daily climb her favorite tree and pray fervently for Jesus to raise her father from the dead the way He had raised Lazarus. She knew all the miracles in her Bible stories, and she believed with all her heart that God would raise her father from the dead and bring him back to her.

Camille's mother was in such deep grief that she was totally unavailable to her. Camille was isolated with her own grief and confusion. Why didn't Jesus raise her father from the dead like Lazarus? Questions flooded her mind, but there was no one to talk to. In the Southern culture of that time people did not talk about their feelings; the proper thing to do was to put on your game face and pretend all was well. Camille wasn't allowed to talk. Her only outlet was her prayers, and God did not answer those.

Unable to cope with her husband's death, Camille's mother vanished into her own private world of drugs and alcohol, the anesthetic for grief prescribed by their family physician. She had never had a drop of alcohol in her life until the doctor prescribed wine in the evenings to help her sleep. This devout Christian mother, who had so carefully schooled Camille in Christianity, began a downhill journey that was unbelievable to Camille and to all who knew her.

In her desperate need for someone to take her dead husband's place, Camille's mother began a relationship with a visiting gospel singer who frequently sang at her church. She was the choir director, so there was ample opportunity to foster this illicit relationship, which eventually led to the breakup of the singer's marriage.

In the process of this sordid turn of events, everything was lost — the family home, the successful business, even the family's reputation in the small Southern town where her father's family had been pillars of the community for generations. Camille's dream turned rapidly into a nightmare.

RUNNING AWAY

Determined to maintain the facade of her life, Camille excelled at school and was very popular. She loved music, literature, art, and escaped into those worlds as often as she could. There was much to run from in Camille's life: her mother's alcoholism, her stepfather's lecherous hands, her lesbian stepsister, the violent fights in the middle of the night, the humiliation of gossip in a small town, and the intense pains that began in her head at the age of twelve.

Her migraine headaches became so severe that Camille would bang her head on the wall and scream in pain. The doctors thought she might have a tumor, or that she was going blind or losing her mind. Undoubtedly, the headaches were a result of the loneliness, fear, insecurity and grief that raged inside of Camille. That internalized rage became the foundation on which she tried to build her life, and the reason for the years of searching and struggle that lay ahead for her.

In an attempt to deaden her headaches, Camille was given prescription drugs at an early age. Not long after this, Camille made her first of many suicide attempts. The intense pain in her head and soul caused her to take an entire bottle of aspirin along with her headache medication. It was not enough to kill her, but at eleven years old it made her seriously sick. She threw up for hours and hours, crawling to the bathroom on hands and knees, with no one to help her.

By this time her mother's illicit relationship with the singer was in full bloom, and she would suddenly take off on weekends to be with him. She would instruct Camille to go stay with her aunt, but there was no way Camille was going to tell her aunt what her mother was doing. She was so ashamed of her mother's behavior that she did everything possible to cover it up. So, she would spend those long weekends by herself, waiting for her mother to return.

Camille began to discover that drugs dulled more than just the physical pain. She became addicted to her prescribed drugs. Her mother never even noticed her drug addiction.

SEARCHING FOR LOVE

Over the next twenty-five years after her father's death, Camille turned – quite naturally – to men, thinking that a man like her father would again fill up that empty space inside which was so dark and vacant since his death. At the young age of sixteen, she married the nicest young man she could find to escape the living hell of her mother's fall from grace.

Obviously, she was ill-equipped to be a wife. Her husband, Paul, sincerely tried to make Camille happy, but thanks to her lecherous stepfather, she was terrified of sex. Six months after her wedding night, her virginity was surgically removed under anesthesia by a sympathetic gynecologist. Unfortunately, the psychic pain remained for Camille.

It was not long before Camille and Paul separated, and after a few months she met Blake. A professional football player, he was quite adept at breaking down all of Camille's inhibitions, using alcohol, drugs and his vast experience with women. Blake swept her off her feet and off to Mexico, where she was divorced from Paul and married to Blake within a matter of moments. Since she spoke no Spanish, she never knew when one marriage ended and the other began.

Blake introduced her to a sophisticated world she had never known before, and they were madly, passionately in love – or so Camille thought. Their life together was one endless party until she became pregnant and no longer attractive to her husband's discerning eye. Then the violent rages began, the verbal, emotional and physical abuse, followed by the tearful apologies.

After giving Blake many warnings, Camille realized his rages were a pattern that would be repeated for the rest of his life. His whole identity had been wrapped up in his football career, and when that ended with an ankle injury, he was lost without the fame and limelight of being a football hero. She realized she would always be his 'whipping boy.' So, with a black eye and a baby boy named Lucas wrapped in her mink coat, she left her sophisticated and exciting new life in the middle of the night, driving as far away from Blake as she could. Little did she realize that she had begun to walk in her mother's footsteps. She, too, was using drugs, alcohol and men as a panacea for her own pain.

When her mother died that year, Camille felt no grief, only relief that for her that chapter was finally closed.

TRYING AGAIN

Three months later, she met her third husband, Ira, who was a very successful, conservative, Jewish businessman from Chicago. More than twenty years older than Camille, he was neither wildly handsome nor exciting, but he was safe, secure, responsible and a non-drinker. She was determined not to make the same mistakes again in choosing a man, and in Ira she felt she had a man she could trust, who would love and adore her and take care of her and her darling Lucas. She thought she had finally found a man like her father.

Her life with Ira was wonderful – at least on the surface. There were furs, jewels, designer clothes, and exotic travel everywhere by private planes and limousines. They had homes in Chicago and Sarasota and a thoroughbred horse farm in Kentucky. Camille became quite the socialite in their international circle of friends. She had a nanny and a housekeeper who both lived in, plus a full-time maid and gardener. Camille had everything she needed.

Then why was she still so miserable? Her headaches and depression remained. Only now she had four different specialists to consult. She was taking so many prescription drugs by this time that she could not eat solid food. Pills were her steady diet. She became anorectic, and for three years her weight did not exceed seventy-two lbs. She practically lived on 'millionaires' row' – the very private top floor of Northwestern Memorial Hospital where Chicago's elite withdrew in the 70s to recuperate from various maladies.

Camille tried every therapy money could buy: Primal scream, Gestalt and Freudian psychoanalysis. You name it, she tried it. Her husband tried. Her doctors tried. The Rabbi tried. Nothing worked. She would swallow a handful of pills, drive her Jaguar at 145 miles per hour, and with tears streaming down her face, scream curses to

God and dare Him to end it all. Death appealed to her more than life.

In this deplorable state of mind, Camille became pregnant. Knowing the fragility of her health, both physically and mentally, her doctors prescribed an abortion, which she had. Three months later she became pregnant again. But this time her husband overrode the advice of the doctors and convinced Camille that fate was dealing the hand. Joshua was born that year on his father's 50th birthday, and the cycle of her anorexia was broken. Nevertheless, Camille remained lonely, bored and depressed. When you have everything you always thought you wanted, and you are still empty inside, an indescribable hopelessness sets in and leaves you worse off than before.

Searching for Life's Meaning

The children were well taken care of by nannies and a housekeeper. Her husband was busy as usual with his endless business deals. Camille felt useless. Was this all that life had to offer? She began studying philosophy and Judaism, and felt a strange pull toward her Jewish roots. Her grandmother was Jewish, though in the Deep South they had managed to keep that quiet, and Camille had converted to Judaism when she married Ira. Now she felt a deep desire to see Jerusalem before she died. Well fortified with anti-depressants, tranquilizers and pain pills, Camille flew to Israel in search of a deeper meaning to life.

She did not find it there, but on the day of her departure she felt strongly drawn to revisit the Western Wall once more. It was a deeply moving sight to Camille – God's chosen people in their orthodox shawls coaxing their tiny scraps of paper with scribbled prayers between the cracks of those ancient temple walls. She stood there with tears in her eyes, wanting with all her heart to believe that there truly was a loving God somewhere.

As a final gesture, Camille scribbled her own prayer and tucked it firmly between the hundreds of others, never realizing the impact that prayer would have on her future.

Dear God,
I can't see you, I can't touch you, I can't hear you. But if you do exist, I need you desperately. Please reveal yourself to me, God,

and it must be in an irrefutable and dramatic way so that I can know without a doubt.

TRAGEDY STRIKES

Camille knows now that this is not a prayer for the faint of heart. Shortly after she prayed it, Joshua was in a drowning accident. The moment of horror is still, years later, frozen in her mind: the piercing scream of the housekeeper, the bloated, rubbery, icy-blue flesh of her 18-month-old son beneath her fingers as she frantically attempted CPR. Time stood still. Kneeling over the lifeless body of her son, Camille prayed the same prayer she had prayed twenty years earlier for her father – that God would bring him back from the dead as He had Lazarus. And if He would, in return she promised to spend the rest of her life seeking Him and serving Him, no matter the cost.

This time the Lord answered her prayer, and somehow she knew irrefutably that God is who He says He is, and since that moment she has never doubted it. She also knew that Joshua would be okay, even though months passed before the doctors confirmed that, and years passed before they determined that he did not have brain damage. The Sarasota newspapers called him 'The Miracle Child.'

Surely this was the irrefutable and dramatic proof she had asked God for in Jerusalem, so it would stand to reason that now Camille would go back to church and become a Christian. But it did not happen that way. Her marriage began to unravel during this highly charged emotional crisis, and despite their love for each other, she and Ira never were able to put it back together again, though through the years they tried.

CONTINUING THE SEARCH

Never being a person of moderation, her promise to God and her spiritual search became paramount, almost an obsession in Camille's life. Once her divorce from Ira was final, her journey through the spiritual alphabet began with astrology and ended with Zen. She lived for a while in a Buddhist monastery in Europe. She moved to South America with the children and studied ancient civilizations for two years. From there her search led to Northern California, where she became a member of the Bear Clan of the Hopi Indian Tribe. Disenchanted after a while, she moved on to a sect of orthodox

Jewish mystics with whom she studied the Cabalah. There is more, but suffice it to say, she left no stone unturned.

Seeking purification of mind and body, she fasted for weeks on water and herbs. She smoked marijuana. She ate psilocybin mushrooms. She took peyote and tripped on LSD through the influence of Harvard's Dr. Timothy Leary and Dr. Richard Alpert. You name it, Camille tried it. These were the formative years of the New Age Movement, and to be a seeker was 'in'. Enlightenment was the goal of this generation, and Camille was swept into all of it.

A LIFE OF BONDAGE

From Jewish American Princess to Jet-set hippy seeker, she was a trendsetter, a connoisseur of the exotic, and the trail was lined with men and drugs. Men, men, men – from a Swedish rock star to a multi-millionaire Texan to a German Count. If only she could find the right man, everything would be fine, she believed. For years Camille was in bondage to her need for pleasure, adventure and the security of a man in her life. Though it may sound glamorous to the uninitiated, the reality was that each of these failed relationships left an emotional scar. God's Word is true. In a sexual union, the two become one. Breaking the bonds of intimacy tears at your very soul, and it creates a bondage like few other sins – a bondage very difficult to break.

FINALLY DELIVERANCE!

It was on the Pacific coast of Northern California that the Lord finally said 'Enough!' Slowly, gently, He began to remove the veil of deception from her eyes. The Lord began to draw her exclusively to Himself through music and books, but most of all through the Bible.

She had a library of occult books that would fill a room. She decided that in order to discover if the Bible were true or not, she should study it and nothing else. So she donated all of her books to the library and concentrated totally on the Bible. From this total concentration, Camille's life began to change drastically. She was miraculously delivered from her lifelong addiction to drugs. She became an avid student of the Bible.

She sought out a teacher and through him became acquainted with a community of Jewish Christian believers. In 1978 she was born into the Kingdom of God and baptized in the Navarro River. She thought her troubles were over, but little did she realize the fury of the enemy who had so long controlled her life. Camille says, 'Once you've experienced the hidden secrets of Satan's kingdom, tasted the exotic fruits of the tree of knowledge, you do not escape easily nor totally unscathed.'

MORE TRIALS AND TESTING

Her ex-husband Ira began to pursue her again during this time. He would alternate between grand gestures of generosity and total refusal to pay child support. These vain attempts to manipulate Camille back into his bed were unsuccessful. Lonely and bitter, he vacillated between pleas and threats, finally becoming so furious that he threatened to have a contract put out on her life. His whole personality changed into someone she had never known before.

She tried to explain to him about her new beliefs and how the Lord had changed her and could change him too. This seemed to make him even angrier. He would ridicule her and warn her that if she persisted, his attorneys could arrange for her to lose everything: Lucas, Joshua, and large sums of money he owed her. Strangest of all, he vowed that he would see her behind bars before it was all over.

Camille did not believe him, but in the end, he made it all happen, right down to the last detail. After seventeen court battles and many thousands of dollars, she lost custody of her son Joshua and was not allowed to see him for two long years. Lucas was sent away to a school in Idaho.

Totally devastated both emotionally and financially, Camille returned to the little school where Joshua had attended third grade, where she once again taught special education. The pain and confusion of teaching and being responsible for other people's children when she was denied her own was almost more than she could bear. Her children had been with her through it all, and now that she was finally capable of being a stable and responsible mother to them, they were gone. This seemed terribly wrong to Camille. Who would teach them about the things of the Lord? How would they ever know the truth? How could God possibly allow this to happen?

THE FINAL HUMILIATION

A few weeks later, a sheriff's deputy came to the school with a warrant for Camille's arrest. Her ex-husband was a man of his word, and he knew that if he did not destroy her completely, she would continue the custody battle indefinitely. So he and his attorneys, with a carefully devised scheme, charged her with fraud against the state of California for having received financial aid during the months he provided child support. It was not true, but he was able to make it appear to be so. Without the prayers of Christian friends and hundreds of character witnesses, she could have easily been sentenced to fourteen years in prison.

At that point, Camille gave up. She learned that whenever you think you've finally lost everything, there is always more. There is your freedom, your reputation, and there is ultimately your own personal sense of who you are. Her attorney, through a series of plea bargains, pled her guilty to a misdemeanor, but she was still sentenced to time in a women's maximum-security state prison. She experienced something very few of us will ever know. She was totally alone in a very hostile and alien place, stripped of her identity, restricted by bars, and called only by a number. That is total humiliation. That will bring you to the very end of yourself.

While there, she led a young woman named Holly to salvation, and like Joseph, what was meant for evil, the Lord used for His good purposes. Eventually Camille became involved in a Christian women's prison ministry in Washington State, but that was years later.

Miraculously, and due to the fervent prayers of other Christian brothers and sisters and a dedicated attorney, Camille was released for 'good behavior' after serving only two weeks of her original sentence. It took years, but ultimately she had her record cleared of those charges – and her heart too. God has so completely removed all the bitterness she had felt toward Ira that she now regularly prays for him.

THE LONG ROAD TO HEALING

When she returned home to her once cozy little beach cottage on the Northern California coastline, she could not bear the loneliness and the memories of her life there with Lucas and Joshua. She would stare out across the ocean for hours, tears streaming down her face wondering, 'Why, Lord? Why does life have to be so hard? And what do you want from me?'

Christian fellowship and Bible studies became her life. There was never an invitation to go forward for prayer that she did not accept. Wherever she went, her Bible went. She clung to the Lord with every ounce of her being because she now knew there was absolutely nowhere else to go.

As Peter had confessed to the Lord centuries earlier, Camille's heart cry was similar: 'Lord, to whom shall we go? You have the words of eternal life' (John 6:68). 'Only Jesus' became her life's theme, and she was learning that when there is nothing more, He is enough. Like Job, she could say, 'Though He slay me, yet will I hope in Him' (Job 13:15). Camille knew the true depth of these words. They were now etched on her heart.

Financially and emotionally depleted, she was invited to move onto the Lord's Land, an old hippy commune transformed into a Jewish Christian community and retreat in Northern California. Her home there was a tiny cabin in the woods with no hot water, an outdoor toilet, and only a wood stove for heat. From the mansion in Florida, she had come a long way, but in those humble surroundings, she received love, instruction, prayer and fellowship that were invaluable to her. She could not have survived the next three years without them. Eventually she became a counselor there and was ordained for ministry. In that position, the Lord gave her the opportunity to touch many lives – prostitutes, people with AIDS, addicts, people deceived by the New Age Movement, homeless people, the brokenhearted. She could identify with them all.

Camille became living proof of God's ability to redeem and heal a broken life. She was healed in all areas except the one she refused to relinquish – her desire for a man in her life. That remained the same. Only one criterion had changed: he had to be a Christian.

DEATH OF A DREAM

Convinced her life was incomplete without marriage, she prayed fervently to convince the Lord of that fact. It was the one idol that still held her in its control. She met Max on the Lord's Land and, having a vision to minister together, they were married. Receiving the blessing, prayer and counsel of their pastor and elders, they moved to Max's hometown in Washington State. Surrounded by his old friends, Max reverted to his former life style, and drugs, alcohol and physical violence re-entered Camille's life. She was devastated. With painful disappointment, the marriage was annulled, and she was left with Max's previous debts to pay and questions that may only be answered when she sees the Lord in heaven. But the marriage idol in her heart was broken forever. Finally.

A LIFE REBUILT

In 1985, Camille returned to Chicago to be near her son, Joshua, during his high school years. Her eldest son, Lucas, joined them shortly thereafter. For years she kept a low profile in Chicago, attending church but avoiding any involvement in ministry. She felt she needed time to sort through the confusion of her failed marriage and reflect on her life in general.

Those years alone with the Lord were time well spent, as He drew her closer and closer to Himself. She has found that when there is only Jesus, He is enough. He is the one she has always longed for. She has found her contentment in Him.

Camille truly embraces her solitary life as a gift from the Lord, and she uses that freedom to devote her time more fully to Him and to her church. Her prayer now is, 'Lord, please don't let it all have been for nothing. Use me to shine your light for others that they may see and no longer walk in darkness; that they may see – and thus glorify our Father in heaven. Then Lord, it will all have been worthwhile.'

God is so patient and long-suffering. People give up long before He does. Camille's story reminds us that the 'Hound of Heaven' just won't quit when He sees a searching heart. It points us once again to that astonishing, mind-blowing, unrelenting grace of our Lord.

14

MY STORY

If you had asked me what I wanted to be when I grew up, I would have said: 'A wife and mother, a musician, a preacher's wife, maybe even a missionary's wife.' But not once would I have said 'a career woman.' That was never even a thought in the back of my mind. Yet for over twenty-five years I have been a career woman. How did that happen? Let me fill you in.

GROWING UP

My traditional Southern family included my parents, two older brothers, and a family dog or bird here or there. My father's nickname for me throughout my childhood was 'hardhead', a tribute to my determination and goal-oriented personality. When I set my head to get something or do something, it was not safe to get in my way. My mother tells of how I could talk my brothers – especially Roger, the middle child – into doing things for me. She would find him bringing me my dolls and toys, grumbling all the while, but somehow unable to tell me 'no'.

My mother was always home for us. She was active in church, but her first priority was her home and children, and that is where she was the happiest. Monday was washing day; Tuesday was ironing day. She had one of those huge sit-down ironers, which she used for all those men's and boys' shirts she laundered every week, after first starching and sprinkling them, rolling them in towels and putting them in the refrigerator overnight. She even ironed sheets.

Most mornings when I got up my mother was studying her Bible. Much of her life she has been a Sunday school teacher for adult women or taught a Bible study in our home. Her greatest love is to study the Bible. She has memorized books and chapters of the Bible through the years, and the Word of God is deeply hidden in her heart.

My dad was a great provider, a very hard worker, and a lot of fun. He always had a wacky sense of humor, and our home was full of laughter because of him. I learned early on to handle teasing, especially about my boyfriends.

I did well in school, mostly due to my competitive spirit and my desire to be 'number one'. My dad was the 'proud father and grandfather' type, and he always believed I could do anything I wanted to do. Embarrassingly, I have heard him tell not a few people that I could have been president of IBM if I had wanted to. He really believed it!

I got along fine with my brothers – well, as fine as brothers and sisters get along. I was three years behind Roger in school, and he would always look out for me. They thought – and probably still think – that I was spoiled because I was the baby and the only girl. That's the way brothers always think. They are now two men I greatly admire and love, with significant accomplishments in their own lives and wonderful families.

Religion was not just a Sunday thing in our home; we went to church three times a week without fail. My parents had become believers as young adults, and they lived their doctrine in our home. Nobody ever had a more normal, loving, nurturing environment in which to grow up than I did.

I accepted Christ into my life as a child in our Baptist church. I remember the tug at my heart as I walked down the church aisle that night; I sincerely wanted to know that I was going to heaven when I died. I had been well taught in Scripture, so I understood what I was doing. I believe that decision I made was genuine.

EARLY ADULTHOOD

After high school I went to a Christian college and majored in music. I could sing pretty well and had always taken piano lessons. I loved music, so that seemed the natural path for me. After all, my goal was to be a homemaker and wife, so music would fit in nicely with my plans.

After two years of college, I married my high school sweetheart, and in order to help him finish his college education, I dropped out of college. It did not bother me at all; I was delighted to walk down that aisle and start my dream of a home and husband.

Our daughter, Julie, was born three years later, and I was thrilled. I put bows and lace and frills on that baby practically before she could open her eyes. This was like 'playing house,' and I enjoyed it immensely.

Moving Away

After graduating with his master's degree, my husband took a job in New York City – of all places! So, we loaded up our Volkswagen Bug and headed out to wild Yankee land when Julie was two. I remember saying good-bye to my parents that day, and Julie kept telling my mother, 'Come on, Mammaw, get in the backseat and come with me.' It was a hard day for all of us, but I was excited about this new adventure, even in wicked New York!

We found a little home in the Westchester suburbs and settled into a nice church, made friends, and life was good. I worked as a secretary for a couple of years so that we could save enough money to buy a house. Housing was terribly expensive in New York compared to Georgia, so that seemed to be a good solution, but it was definitely just a temporary job in order to save some money for a down payment.

When Julie was entering first grade, my husband took an overseas assignment with his company. Because of the difficult living conditions in that country, he was not allowed to bring his family, so he was away for the better part of a year. I decided to go back to college and complete my degree since it was no longer necessary for me to work. So, Julie and I went off to school each day, and I completed my degree in music. I also became the music director for our church, and it was more fun than I had ever imagined. I loved it!

Drastic Changes

When Julie was eight years old, I found myself going through a divorce. The separation had not been good for our marriage, and it set the stage for this split. The causes were many, as is usually the case, and sadly I lost my will to try to put the marriage back together. Nothing could have been more foreign to my plans, my beliefs or my self-image. Nothing could have been more devastating to my family.

This put me in the situation of having to find a job, and I had a degree in music! I applied to IBM, where I had worked previously as a secretary, and was hired as one of their first female sales reps. Overnight I was thrust into a world for which I was totally unprepared. It was a world full of men – lots of impressive men, and I was easily caught up in that world. I was very insecure about myself as a woman at that point, very needy in many ways, and there was a lot of pressure on me. Pressure to succeed in this new career; pressure to be a good mother to Julie and try to make up to her for the divorce; pressure to prove I was okay. And to me that meant I had to find a man.

A DESPERATE DECADE

With all the good teaching I had had and all my Bible knowledge, you would think I would have leaned on the Lord and trusted Him at this point in my life. I needed Him then more than ever. But my hardheadedness led me in the wrong direction then, for I became determined to find an earthly man who could validate me and make me feel worthwhile.

I was in a man's world, so there were men in my life. They were men I met in business, because our small suburban church had no single men my age. I knew what the Bible taught about divorce; I knew God hated it. I thought He would punish me for being divorced by making me be single forever, and I was determined not to let that happen to me.

So, little by little, I began to take control of my life and guide it in the direction I wanted it to go. I wanted to be accepted in my new world, and I didn't want to jeopardize any potential relationships by being too religious. I blended in well with my peers, and had you known me on the job then, I think you would have been surprised to hear me say that I was a committed Christian. Of course, I never would have told you that, and indeed I backed away from my Christian commitment.

I never stopped going to church, but I began to lead a double life. The standards and principles in which I had believed and lived all my life were compromised one by one. We rarely take giant leaps away from God; it usually comes in baby steps, and that was true for me.

Looking for Mr. Right

Though it probably appeared to most people as though I had my act together during those years, inside I was a fearful woman, afraid of being single forever. I thought that if I could find the man, that special man who met all my criteria, he would bring meaning, love and fulfillment to what seemed to me an empty existence. I spent many sleepless nights wondering why Prince Charming had not come along yet, wondering when and if he ever would, wondering what was wrong with me.

Many times, as a single woman, I carefully thought through the qualities and characteristics that I was looking for in a man. After many hours of analysis, I knew exactly what I wanted in a man; what I could not live without and what I would like to have but would be willing to compromise on. Had you asked me, I would have easily recited to you a clear, concise description of the personality traits and distinctive features of my ideal man. Of course, as the years passed, I became more and more willing to lower those standards and accept someone far less than my ideal, as long as he was a man! My guess is some of you know exactly what I mean.

But here is what I was looking for in a man.

- *First, I wanted a man who would love me more than I loved him.* I worked with a single friend, and we shared our thoughts about men, as single women are prone to do. I remember her saying to me, 'You know, Mary, it is much better in a relationship if the man is just a little more in love than the woman. If a woman can just believe that this man in her life loves her a little bit more than she loves him, it makes for a better relationship.'

  I thought about that and decided what she really was saying was that most women 'flip' too quickly over a man, and if they don't scare him off, they place themselves in a very weak position in the relationship. He knows she is crazy about him, and she begins to think she is so lucky just to have him. The relationship seems to get out of balance from the beginning, and she is 'more in love' than he is.

  Ever notice that? Well, I decided that I did not want that to happen to me, so one of my objectives was to find a man who loved me a little more than I loved him – or at least to let him think that he did.

- *I wanted a man who truly understood me.*

  Let's face it, we all know that women and men think differently. Our logic, which is so clear, concise and correct to us, is frequently lost on the men in our lives. Though they may try to understand us, there is frequently that bit of a gap, and there are times when no amount of communication seems to be able to bridge it. Yet I was convinced that somewhere I could find a man who would understand how I thought and really get inside my head and my heart. That was what I was looking for.

- *I wanted a relationship that was totally secure.*

  I think all women share this strong desire. We like to know that our love will last, that nothing will ever cause it to disintegrate. If you have ever experienced a broken relationship, you know how your girlhood dreams of 'happily ever after' have been shattered. Perhaps you have become cynical about relationships and about men, believing that no man can be trusted, or that no relationship is secure. I was determined to find a man who would never leave me, never find anyone he liked better than me – never even look!

- *I wanted a man who would be my best friend.*

  I had made up my mind that this was a requirement that could not be compromised. The man in my life had to be my best friend, someone interested in every detail of my life, eager to hear about things that interested me, happy to share good times with me, to laugh with me, to cry with me, to offer advice when needed.

- *I wanted a gentle but strong man.*

  I wonder if most women share my desire to find this kind of gentle, but strong man. It is a rare combination and not easy to locate, but it is a marvelous trait to find in a man. My man would be secure enough about his manhood to be gentle, not afraid to show vulnerability or softness, shed a few tears openly at times, and no longer have to prove to anyone that he is a man. At the same time, he would be steel on the inside, decisive, smart, action-oriented.

- *I wanted a man with the 'right looks.'*

  While most of us would have different opinions as to what makes a man good looking, it is still fairly certain that a man's looks are important to us. Are we proud to be seen with him? Does he dress well? Does he carry himself well? We all have certain ideas of what the man in our life should look like, and I was no exception. It was a certain air, a presence – I knew it when I saw it!

ON THE MOVE AGAIN

So, I searched for Mr. Right while keeping the career going and trying to be a good mom. When there was a relationship in my life that I thought had promise, I was flying high and that became my highest priority. When those relationships went sour or died natural deaths, I would say, 'Who needs men?' and pour myself into the career, getting another promotion, buying more clothes, trying to fill up the void inside of me.

Julie and I moved to Princeton, New Jersey, when she was a freshman in high school, as I took a promotion with IBM. Then when she was entering her junior year, I left IBM and took a job in Chicago. It was probably the most foolish decision I ever made in most ways. What single mother would unnecessarily move her teenage daughter to a large, strange city as a junior in high school? Why would a smart woman leave a secure job that held much promise with a company like IBM? Why would anyone go to a big city where she knew no one and would have to start over again, if she did not have to?

Why? Because I thought surely in a big city like Chicago I could find a man. I figured that my mistake had been to live in the suburbs where there were few single men to be found. I thought that by living and working in a big city atmosphere, the likelihood of meeting single men would greatly increase.

Of course, I told everyone that I was moving for a new job opportunity. Another good company had offered me this job, and I convinced myself it offered rare potential and was too good to be refused. But underneath I knew that I had moved in desperation. Several hopeful relationships had gone under, and I was truly worried that I would be single forever.

So, we moved into a nice rehabbed condominium on the North side of Chicago. Julie got settled into a private school and adjusted well, and I started falling apart.

PLANS GONE AWRY

The job turned out to be a bust. I was stuck with no options, and I was by myself without family or friends in this big city. But with my hardheaded attitude, I did not give up easily. I simply doubled my efforts to find that man and tried everything I could to make the job work.

A good description of me at this point would be an emotional 'yo-yo'. I was up and down, depending on how the job was going or if there was some hope for a new relationship. However, the lows seemed to be more frequent and more pronounced all the time. Mary was losing control.

A BRIEF REPRIEVE

Then, into my life came a nice man, a really nice man. I thought finally I had paid my dues and it was my time. He had the prestige, the looks, the personality I was looking for, and he seemed to genuinely care for me.

But soon I recognized that, while he really liked me and this could possibly develop at some point into a permanent relationship, this nice man was not ready to make any commitments. He had just come out of a divorce and wisely decided to take it slowly. So, while I was pushing and hoping and dying for a commitment, he was being cautious and careful.

The 'yo-yo' started again. When I felt the relationship was making progress, I was fine. Otherwise, I could not sleep, eat, think, work or do anything very well. I had found a new job, but it certainly did not fill up the void inside me. I wanted this man, and that was all there was to it.

During all this period, my spiritual life was down to nothing. I never read my Bible, never prayed, and tried to stay so busy that I could squash the nagging, convicting voice of God inside of me. Remember, I was determined to get married again, and I was not going to let God get in my way.

AT THE END OF THE ROPE

One night I felt such desperation that I did what would appear to be a very stupid thing. I can remember feeling as though I almost had no control over what I was doing, wondering why I was doing it, but unable to stop.

I got up shortly after midnight, not being able to sleep, dressed, and went to my friend's home to break off our relationship. I knocked on his door, woke him up, and we talked for a few hours. It was a weird conversation because I had no reason to end the relationship and could never give him a good answer as to why. Nothing had happened between us to precipitate this action; he had done nothing wrong. All I could tell him was, 'I just can't handle it anymore.'

Maybe I thought I could get to him through this drastic action; maybe I just had to do something to feel I was in control. I am not really certain, because I was not thinking clearly at all at this point. As I left his home early that morning, he asked when he could call me. I remember saying, 'Don't call me. I'll call you.'

REACHING FOR A LIFELINE

I went back to my home and for about the first time in ten years, I found my Bible and began to read God's Word. For three days I was a zombie and unable to sleep. I knew that I had to make a decision about my commitment to Jesus Christ. I knew I could no longer straddle the fence as I had done for ten years. I also knew that whatever I decided, it had to be once and for all. I was sick of being a hypocrite. I was tired of the 'yo-yo' life, and I wanted peace more than anything else.

Finally, after three days of reading and some desperate praying, I said to God what had to be said: 'Lord, I'll do anything You want me to do. I'll be anything You want me to be, if only You will give me peace. I'll even be single forever.'

It would be difficult to describe how painful those words were for me to say. I knew that I was not fooling around with God anymore and this was serious. I still thought that being single was the worst thing in the world and that my life would be miserable, but at least I would have some peace with God. It was warped thinking, but it was all I was capable of at the time.

When I finally released my clenched fists, I found that wonderful peace with God that had been missing for all those years. That came instantly with confession of sin and my willingness to finally turn the reins of my life over to the Lord. It was so refreshing to have the lines open between me and God again. What blessed joy to get rid of the ton of guilt I had carried for so long and to know His forgiveness! Peace like a river flooded my soul immediately, and I was hooked. That peace had been missing for ten years, and I knew I could never exist again without it.

REBUILDING AND RELEARNING

There was no overnight miracle, however. I had the peace, but the pain of watching my dream die did not go away In fact, it seemed to get worse. For reasons I do not now remember, I started writing in a journal at that time, and so from my journals I can retrace my progress and remember the process I underwent as I gave God control of my life.

There were days when I wrote in my journal, 'I don't think I'm going to make it.' Or, 'Today is worse than yesterday.' But the pain of relinquishment drove me to the Word of God and to daily communication with Him. I began to get up earlier and earlier in order to have enough time with Him at the beginning of my day. Not because I was trying to be a good Christian, but because I could not make it through the day without the strength and comfort He gave me in those morning hours.

God began a new work in my heart that continues to this day. For an intensive 18-month period, I struggled with letting go of my dream to be married. I was frequently tempted to call my friend, knowing that he was likely to be receptive to re-establishing our relationship. Many times I dialed his number with that intention, only to hear the quiet voice of God's Spirit saying inside of me, 'Can't you trust Me?' Then I would hang up with tears, and say, 'Yes, Lord, I can trust You. I will trust You.'

I began to learn to trust a trustworthy God. I began to get to know God. How thankful I am for all the teaching I had in my life, for it was sitting there in my mind, a ready resource for growth. I became active in my church, Moody Memorial Church in Chicago, where I had attended since moving to Chicago. My pastor, Dr. Erwin Lutzer, was and is such a blessing in my life through his sermons and through his encouragement.

I well remember the night when I knew I had made it through the worst and would no longer be tortured with this desire for marriage. I had agreed to have dinner with this man I had wanted so badly, just a friendly get-together after all these months, but as I sat with him at dinner that evening, it was as though the blinders fell off and I could see that behind all the nice exterior, this man was more insecure than I ever realized. After all, he did not know Jesus, and I saw that we had little in common now. Conversation was difficult to keep going, and though I tried to share my new life with him, it was as though I spoke a foreign language that he could not understand.

I walked away from that evening saying, 'Thank You, Jesus, for sparing me from my own desires.' I realized, as I walked down that Chicago street (I remember exactly which it was), that I was no longer a slave to that desire. I was free to be God's woman, whatever that turned out to be, and life would indeed be good. I was not doomed to misery. I thought that, had I been cured of cancer, it could not have been a greater miracle. And that is the truth. The difference between the 'yo-yo' woman I was and the new, free woman I was becoming in Christ was the biggest miracle I could imagine. I knew I could never change me, and yet I was changed.

A New Man in my Life

One particular morning during this 18-month transition period, I read Mark 15, and my thoughts were captured by something I had never noticed before. This chapter depicts the mockery of a trial that was given to our Lord and also His death on the cross. In verse 40, after Jesus had uttered His last cry, we read:

> Some women were watching from a distance. Among them were Mary Magdalene, Mary the mother of James the younger and of Joses; and Salome. In Galilee these women had followed Him and cared for His needs. Many other women who had come up with Him to Jerusalem were also there.

I began to understand that Jesus had a particular magnetism for women in His day. They followed Him wherever He went: on long dusty journeys, in a day when travel was difficult and women were not accepted as equals; in a day when their decision to follow Jesus must have been viewed as particularly improper and foolish. Yet Mark tells us that many women followed Jesus.

They were there at the cross, when most of the disciples had fled. They were there enduring with Him His disgrace and His suffering. They were there to anoint His dead body and they were at the tomb, the first to come back and mourn His death. These women were totally captivated by the Man, Jesus Christ.

The eyes of my understanding started to open up that morning as the Inner Voice said to me, 'He was the Man in their lives, and they were women just like you, no different. He can be the Man in your life too.'

Then I remembered my list – all those requirements I had established for the man in my life. A flood of understanding poured over me, and I saw how totally Jesus met all my qualifications. I had trusted Him as my Savior long ago, but that morning I accepted Him as the Man in my life.

Remember my list?

- *I wanted a man who would love me more than I loved him.*

  Well, I have found Him. Jesus loves me more than I could ever love Him. In John 15:9 Jesus said, 'As the Father has loved Me, so have I loved you.' It is not possible for our human minds to comprehend the way the Father loved the Son, but try to expand your mind a bit and grasp this truth.

  I have not found that earthly man, but may I tell you that the love my Lord Jesus has for me is so abundant, so rich, so completely satisfying, that it is beyond description. There's absolutely no doubt about it: He loves me more than I will ever be able to love Him.

  More than that, the quality of His love is pure. He does not love me because He needs me, or because He likes my looks, or because I meet His requirements. He does not love me because I love Him, nor does He love me because I am easy to love. He does not give or take away His love based on how I perform. He will never love me more than He does now because He loves me totally.

  I have found Him: the Man, and the only Man, who does and will always love me more than I love Him.

- *I wanted a man who truly understood me.*

Jesus understands me better than anyone else. He understands my personality. My actions don't catch Him by surprise. He is not puzzled by anything I say or do. I never leave Him shaking His head and saying, "What in the world goes on inside that woman's head?"

In fact, He understands me far better than I understand myself. Many times He has revealed to me things about myself which I never could figure out. Many times He has put the pieces in place in my own personality puzzle, and helped me to see why I am like I am and why I do what I do.

He knows my thoughts, so I don't have to keep trying to explain things to Him. The Bible tells me that He has searched me and known me and understands my thoughts from afar (Ps. 139:1-2).

Just recently I was struggling over an issue and found myself unable to verbalize how I felt to the Lord. Finally, I said, 'Oh, Lord, You know how I am!' And He gave me that quiet assurance that indeed He knows exactly how I am. He can read between my lines and translate my emotions, which is often more than I can do.

- *I wanted a relationship that was totally secure.*

Jesus has promised that He will never leave me or forsake me – never – and He cannot lie. Losing my beauty (what there is of it) or my youth (what there is left) won't ever cause Him to leave me. If I were to become ill or handicapped, He would not leave me. There will never be anyone to win His attentions away from me.

No one else can make us that promise. Even a good man in a good marriage can only promise us 'til death do us part', but nothing can separate me from the love I have in Christ Jesus. If you think 'happily ever after' only exists in storybooks, you should get to know Jesus Christ.

- *I wanted a man who would be my best friend.*

Jesus truly is the best friend I have – the friend who cares about all the details, who rejoices when something good happens to me, who cries with me when I'm sad. He is a wonderful friend.

153

I remember when it first began to dawn on me that Jesus was my best friend. At one point during this transition period, I was going through a difficult time with my job, and I so wanted to talk to someone about it. While I bored a few of my friends with some details, I hesitated to dump the whole mess on them.

One day was particularly tough, and I had shed a few tears in the privacy of my office. At home that night by myself (Julie was now in college), I started my pity party all over again. I rethought the terrible day and wished so much that I just had someone to talk to, someone who would listen to every little detail and let me really get it out of my system.

As I wallowed in this pity, I remembered the tears I had shed that day over the situation. I could feel them trickling down my cheeks again. While I was thinking that nobody really cared about my tears, I remembered that verse in Psalm 56:8 (KJV) which says, 'Thou tellest my wanderings; put Thou my tears into Thy bottle; are they not in Thy book?' I realized that those silly, insignificant tears I had shed were in His bottle. God was fully aware of them, He understood them. They were important to Him – so important that He put them in His bottle.

I came out of my self-pity rather quickly as I acknowledged that I had the best friend in all the world to share my problems, big and small, one who never gets tired of hearing all my nitty-gritty details, one who is never too busy or preoccupied to listen to my requests and give me help. He happens to be the Creator of all the Universe, the King of kings and Lord of lords. But He is also my best friend, Jesus Christ.

- *I wanted a gentle but strong man.*

Jesus is the ultimate Gentle-Man. The only personality description He ever gave of Himself was that He was 'gentle and humble in heart' (Matt. 11:29). We know that He endured everything we will ever have to endure on this earth. Every possible kind of temptation that we will ever face, He encountered, though He never sinned. Because He has walked this road before us, we are told that He is 'touched with the feeling of our infirmities' (Heb. 4:15, KJV). He sympathizes with our weaknesses.

When He deals with me, He uses such incredible gentleness that I can handle whatever He says. At just the right moment, He quietly drops a thought or suggestion into my mind, or a rebuke, to show me where I need to improve, what needs changing in my life. Because of His marvelous gentleness, I don't resent His dealings with me, and I really want to change whatever it is that displeases Him. Gentle – oh my, yes! Only He could be so gentle.

Jesus, however, was never weak. He attacked the evil institutions of His day without mincing one word. He addressed the religious hypocrites with unequaled directness. He never lacked backbone or decisiveness.

Yet where there was the slightest inclination on anyone's part to know Him, He dealt with them with compassion and kindness and gentleness. Remember the woman caught in adultery? Quietly, gently He spoke with her; He had compassion on her, yet He directly confronted her sin, without condemnation and without guilt trips. He deals with people with directness, love and gentleness.

This Man, Christ Jesus, is the perfect combination of gentleness and strength. If you thought that was impossible to find, I'd like you to meet Him. You won't be disappointed.

- *I wanted a man with the 'right looks.'*
I have discovered that, as the psalmist says, Jesus is 'fairer than the children of men' (Ps. 45:2, KJV). He said Himself that He is the bright Morning Star (Rev. 22:16). He is described as altogether lovely, the rose of Sharon, the lily of the valley. I can tell you that His beauty is unsurpassed. Though I've not yet seen His face, He is real to me and my heart 'sees' Him. He is truly fairer than any earthly man could be, as nice as they are. Someday I will see His face, and I know that He will be more beautiful than my dreams and imagination of Him.

Yes, indeed, there is a Man in my life. It has been more than twenty-three years since I came back to God and gave Him control over my life, and I'm still totally single! In fact, there has been no earthly man in my life during all these years, but this Man continues to be all and more than I ever wanted in a man.

A NEW LIFE

In these past years God has chosen to demonstrate in me how beautiful His Plan B can be. I made a mess of Plan A, but He is such a great God that even the second best is beyond belief.

I began working in my church and started caring about other people. That is the first step to healing, I believe, and even during my painful transition period, I was able to reach out to many others. I started a small Bible study in my home on Monday evenings for a few close friends, and that continued for several years. What a support group that was for me, and how I love those women to this day.

Then I started a monthly ministry at my church for workplace women, recognizing there were many women like me in this urban church who worked outside their homes and, like me, they needed help and encouragement. That monthly luncheon continues and is the foundation of all my ministry. It is home-base for me, and God has used it in ways I can't even begin to comprehend. I now have the privilege of serving on the staff of my church as Director of Women's Ministries.

During this time I noticed that there were no programs on Christian radio directed to workplace Christians, and I began to pray about that need. It was one of those prayers that makes you feel foolish when you mouth the words, because it seems so far out in left field. In fact, I didn't even tell anyone I was praying about a radio program because I knew it would sound crazy.

One day, on the way to work, I thought, 'You've been praying about this for many months now; maybe it's time you did something about it. I wonder how you begin a radio program?' I decided then to put some kind of a sample program together and try to get it on the air, and that was all I knew about radio!

That very day I received an invitation to be a guest panelist on a new Christian radio station in Chicago. It came out of the blue, and I didn't think it was a coincidence. After I finished the program with them a few days later, I told them about my idea for a radio program and asked how I could get it on the air. They encouraged me, gave me some advice, and I started to work on a program.

That was in May of 1984, and by August we were on the air with a fifteen-minute Saturday program called, 'The Christian Working Woman.' From that we expanded to other stations and additional formats, so that now the program is broadcast in three formats on over 500 Christian stations across the country and internationally. Who would ever have guessed? Certainly not me!

Having to continually write for the radio program led me to write a few books, and from all of that have come invitations to speak to many groups.

My life is not trouble-free or perfect. I still struggle with all kinds of issues, like everyone else, but no longer am I in bondage to my idol of marriage. I have discovered the real joy and contentment of allowing Jesus to be the Man in my life, and I can honestly say that if I'm single forever it's not only okay with me, it suits me just fine!

HE'S AVAILABLE FOR YOU

If you have never really known Jesus personally, I urge you to get to know Him. For though He is the Man in my life, He's totally capable of being the Man in your life, too.

He said, 'Come to Me, all you who are weary and burdened, and I will give you rest' (Matt. 11:28). You can be absolutely certain of His acceptance, because He said that anyone who comes to Him, He will never drive away (John 6:37). In order to come to Him in this personal relationship, you must acknowledge that you are a sinner. You cannot save yourself by good works or living a good life, and without His redemption and forgiveness, you are lost. Once you confess your sins and accept His salvation, you become a member of the family, a child of God, born anew.

You may be wondering, 'How do you know the presence of Jesus in your life when He is not a flesh-and-blood person living on the earth? How does He speak to you? How do you experience His love and understanding?' I've told the story of the little boy who was scared of the dark, but his father said to him, while tucking him in bed, 'Now, son, don't be scared when I turn the lights out. Remember, Jesus is always here with you.' His son replied, 'Yes, but I want someone with skin on.'

Is that how you feel sometimes? I understand. Those are normal feelings. But I want to assure you that even though Jesus doesn't have 'skin on' right now, or at least we're not able to see it, He can be more real to you, more satisfying to you than any earthly relationship.

How do we get to know Him? Well, the best way is through the Bible, which was written so that we could know who Jesus is, why He came to earth, and what He offers us. By reading, meditating and memorizing Scripture, I'm getting to know Him very well. Through prayer I talk to Him, just as I would to you. The more I yield my mind to Him, the more He uses my thoughts to convey His thoughts to me. As time passes, I am becoming more and more conscious of His presence in every part of my life, and He is able to communicate with me personally, through His Word and through His Spirit.

Whether you are married or single, whether you have a man in your life or not, you will soon learn, if you have not already, that no other person on earth can completely meet your needs. We women tend to think that when we find and marry the 'right' man, our search for satisfaction and completeness has ended. But regardless of how wonderful that earthly man is, he will not be able to fill the void inside you which was put there by God – that Jesus-shaped void which only He can completely fill.

No More Parched Ground

At one point I remember reading a passage from Isaiah 41:18:

> I will make rivers flow on barren heights, and springs within the valleys. I will turn the desert into pools of water, and the parched ground into springs.

I thought of how the Lord had taken the parched ground of my life and given me springs of water. But I felt guilty, because I knew I didn't deserve it. I said to the Lord, 'You know, Lord, much of my problem was my own fault. I don't deserve Your grace and acceptance because I knew better.' So gently, that quiet inaudible voice of God's Spirit said to me, 'I delight to turn your parched ground into springs, even when you are the one who set the fire that caused the desolation.'

This, Mary's story, is truly one of astonishing grace! By all rights God should have put me on the shelf and let me rot there. Even if He took me back, He had every right to hold it over my head, berate and punish me, and make an example of me. I was a woman who had no excuses for the selfish life I led for so long. Unlike many of the other stories in this book, I knew God, and I knew better.

Yet He has chosen instead to make me an example of His grace by demonstrating how He can use the most useless, unqualified, undeserving person you can imagine. No one is more amazed than I am at what God's grace has done in my life. My greatest joy is to be able to share with other women that while you can blow it so badly, or miss the mark so widely, or stray so far from God, He is always able to salvage your life and turn your ashes into beauty.

That is because He is a God of grace. I hope that you will never ever forget it, and that you will live in the radiance of His astonishing grace!